Riding

FROM THE

Inside Out

for
Nigel

First published in the United States of America in 2005
by Trafalgar Square Publishing
North Pomfret, Vermont 05053

First published in Australia in 2003 by Lisa Champion
First published in Great Britain 2005

Printed by Midas Printing International Limited, China

Disclaimer of Liability
The authors and publisher shall have neither liability nor responsibility to any
person or entity with respect to any loss or damage caused or alleged to be
caused directly or indirectly by the information contained in this book. While the
book is as accurate as the authors can make it, there may be errors, omissions,
and inaccuracies.

ISBN 1-57076-324-0

Library of Congress Control Number: 2005901884

Photography © Julieann Howard

Photography © Roz Neave
p 6, Shane Rose and Never on Sunday 2002
p 7, Ricky MacMillan and Crisp 2003
p 51, Vicki Roycroft and Luna Luna 2002
p 103, Lisa Wilcox and Relevant 2002

Designed by Ingo Voss, vossdesign and Paul Saunders

Disclaimer
Please treat your body safely. The exercises contained in this book are
designed for healthy individuals. Consult your doctor or physiotherapist if you
are concerned about your ability to undertake an exercise program without
compromising your health.

Riding
FROM THE
Inside Out

Lisa Champion

Anna-Louise Bouvier

With riding insights by Larissa Chadwick

Trafalgar Square Publishing
North Pomfret, Vermont

Contents

part one
Balanced riding

part two
Grounded riding

part three
Soft riding

part four
Lifelong riding

why do we love to ride?

We ride because we love horses. For centuries there has been a special bond between people and horses and the sense of harmony with another creature that we sometimes experience while riding is a deeply satisfying feeling.

We ride because we love the challenge of mastering a complex skill. Riding looks so natural, but it is very difficult to do well and we are constantly striving to improve our abilities in the saddle.

And we ride because it is such an exhilarating and exciting thing to do.

We all recognise highly skilled riding when we see it. There is nothing as inspiring as watching a great rider smoothly taking a huge jump or performing a near-perfect dressage test. Excellent riding seems like an effortless combination of beauty and balance and excellent riders have a gift for bringing the horse to them. They have complete control over every action and the horse responds perfectly to their directions. It all looks so natural. Horse and rider work seamlessly together as a single entity and that is the essence of good riding.

Meanwhile, back at home most of us are only too aware that we are a long way off being outstanding riders. We find that improvements are very hard won, despite our efforts. Maybe your legs and feet don't cooperate while you're on the horse. Or you feel that you never have him in the right shape, no matter what you try. Or you're always too stiff in the sitting trot. Or your shoulders and arms are always tense.
Or… If you're a rider, you know your own shortcomings. It's frustrating to keep on trying to improve without fully understanding what you are doing wrong. What you're trying to do is to finally unlock the secret of easy, natural, graceful riding.

riding tall

The single element that unites all the various horse riding techniques is good posture. Put simply: good posture is the secret of good riding.

Instructors emphasise that to ride well means having an independent seat and effective leg aids with subtle rein aids and all this relies on a strong, stable centre. On the other hand, most inefficient riding styles can be attributed to poor posture. If you're struggling to improve your riding efficiency, the chances are you need to improve your posture.

This is not as straightforward as it may at first appear. There is more to good posture than pulling your tummy in or your shoulders down. It's about:

- identifying your postural type
- becoming aware of ingrained motor patterns
- bringing about permanent changes in your body.

Most of all it's about changing the way you do things off the horse before you can apply them while you're on the horse.

And it's about assuming responsibility for your body and the way it moves and responds, rather than expecting your riding instructor to fix you.

It's up to you

Taking responsibility for your posture and movement habits entails making a serious commitment to change ingrained patterns. These patterns feel intuitively right to you now, but only because you have been doing them for a very long time. New movement patterns will feel strange and won't become habit easily because your body will want to return to what is familiar, even when you know it's not good for you. The benefits of persisting in trying to change are worth the effort as you'll feel, look and ride taller. You'll also help to counteract the effects gravity has on the body as we age.

Riding from the Inside Out is a complete guide to posture for riders. It provides a series of riding-specific exercises and posture cues de-veloped by an innovative physiotherapist that will retrain your body. It will also help you to think about your riding in a whole new way, one that is guaranteed to make you the better, more natural rider you want to be. All you need is about 20 minutes a day and some persistence and belief in your body's ability to change and you will discover new levels of mastery in your riding.

You will learn to love riding even more.

Lisa's story

I am a fitness professional. I have a master's degree in exercise science and have worked in the fitness industry for 20 years. I have taught group fitness classes, worked as a personal trainer, presented workshops at international conventions and I am a trainer of trainers. I've also been a keen athlete, competing in triath-lons and marathons. Even after having four children, my body has stayed trimmed, toned and strong.

So, when I took up dressage riding five years ago I assumed that my substantial exercise history would allow me to become a pretty good rider in no time flat. I soon realised that all the strength and fitness in the world were not what I needed to be effective on the horse. I just couldn't get it and I didn't know what I was doing wrong. It was very frustrating. After all, I was motivated, fit, committed, analytical and knowledgeable—how hard could this be? Little did I realise that the answer lay in thinking about my body in a way that was completely outside my experience until then.

I was fortunate to find the brilliant dressage coach Larissa Chadwick and we continue to train two or three times a week. Over those early months we carefully unpicked what was happening in my body. Session after session, she would point out how tense I was and instruct me to relax. Intellectually I knew what I had to do, but the harder I tried the more tense I became. I couldn't let go of the tension in my limbs and 'just relax'. I worked hard at producing a quality of softness in my riding, although it became increasingly clear that the softness I was looking for is the product of intuition and skill rather than strength and determination. My fitness background was helping to an extent, but there was a still a piece missing.

I turned for advice to my friend Anna-Louise Bouvier, the most out-of-the-square physiotherapist you can imagine. Her gift is for im-proving posture and developing sport-specific exercises to either stretch or strengthen different body parts, depending upon the body's habitual responses and the skill or movement required. She didn't know much about riding but was still able to provide startling insights into the problems I was experiencing. My essential difficulties lay not in what I was doing on the horse but in my posture. I was astounded as I took it for granted that, as a fitness person, I had great posture.

So, the three heads combined—the coach, Larissa, with her skill and knowledge of riding technique, the student, me, with my determination to improve and the physiotherapist, Anna-Louise, with her specialised analysis of muscle and movement. Between us we de-vised a revolutionary approach to enhance riding technique.

I have learned many things about my body along the way and I am anxious to share what I have learned with other struggling, frustrated, eager students. Take it from me. While my journey to become a better rider is still on-going, I can honestly say that I have improved enormously—proof of just how effective *Riding from the Inside Out* can be.

Larissa's story

Larissa Chadwick has achieved the dream shared by thousands of young riders around the country—taking a horse from Pony Club to Grand Prix dressage.

Larissa started riding at the age of four and became a member of the Cobbity Pony Club when she was six. When she was 10, her mother, Patricia, bought a three-year-old Morgan horse, Brandy (Aura Dell Alexander). They were to form a lasting partnership. 'From the first moment Brandy and I rode together I have never once felt scared or unsure. We clicked from the start and I have always felt that there was nothing we couldn't do,' she says.

By the time she was 12, Larissa had chosen dressage as her preferred riding discipline and Patricia began looking for the right trainer to assist her development. They decided upon Vickie Robertson, who went on to work with Larissa and Brandy for over 10 years.

Still at the age of 12, Larissa won the Pony Club NSW State Dressage Championships in the under-13 age group. By the time she was 14, she had entered her first official Dressage Council (DC) competition. By 15 she was riding Prix St George level and she competed at Grand Prix when she was 22. For the last seven years of their career (up until 2000), she and Brandy were among the top 12 dressage riders in the country. She is now a professional rider and trainer who teaches riding full-time while training and competing horses for various clients. She has also spent time overseas, improving her skills and broadening her know-ledge of and experience in the dressage world.

Larissa is a natural born talent—an artist on the horse. She has the ability to feel what is happening in the horse's body and to bring out the best in each one she rides. She is in that top 5% of riders who naturally have a stable core. Years of correct training have built upon and refined her natural talent. The result is a rider who is effective, balanced, strong and soft, all at the same time. When one of Australia's leading teachers of the Alexander Technique, Mary Cerny, watched Larissa ride, she commented, 'She has a complete connection between the top of her head and the soles of her feet.'

Larissa also has the rare ability to see what is happening in the bodies of her students as they ride. She believes in teaching her students how to use themselves in a balanced way, thereby enabling the horse to balance itself better.

Larissa says

So much of what I see when teaching my students is a mirroring of the movement habits of the rider in the movement patterns of the horse. If a person is really stiff, the horse tends to be stiff. If a person is quite sloppy or slumps, the horse ends up moving in a similar way.

When I am riding, I am always searching for a balance between softness in my body with stability and correctness in my position. I then wait and encourage the horse to mould his body around my correct position. I see many students trying to lean, push, pull, collapse and move excessively and then expect their horse to perform perfect school shapes. By looking at the simplest lines—shoulder-hip-heel; elbow-wrist-bit; shoulders level; hips level—I can see how my students need to improve. I encourage them to think of how much their body position and stillness can influence the horse. This is not as easy as it sounds, because without the correct riding posture it's really difficult to get a horse truly forward with all the right elements in place—not to mention with beauty as well.

I have been greatly influenced by my experiences overseas, especially with Wolfram Wittig in Germany. He is an incredibly balanced rider who never seems to waiver in his postural integrity.

I returned home with such a clear image of how German trainers ride, how they sit and what they ask of their horses and I want my students to have a small glimpse of the balance and forward I was able to feel on Wittig's horses.

Riding on magnificent horses from one of the world's best stables is out of reach for most riders, but the skill to ride with strength and integrity is something that is available to anyone who wants to try. We have a long way to go in Australia towards improving our riding positions, but the work I have done with Lisa and Anna-Louise contributes to helping us all achieve balance with beauty. It is worth pointing out that the exercises for us humans in this book often reflect the exercises I get the horses to do under saddle. The suppling, correct positioning and degree to which I bend or straighten is all like doing active physiotherapy for the horse.

If you are trying to improve your own riding, my words of encouragement are:
- trust your body
- work on getting honest feedback on what you can improve
- do the exercises off the horse
- when you get in the saddle, believe that if your position is correct it will encourage your horse to be balanced and move more correctly.

a new way to think about riding

The exercises and strategies devised for me by Anna-Louise Bouvier are based on the method of exercise-therapy she has developed called Physiocise. This method has helped hundreds of sufferers of chronic back pain and can be adapted brilliantly to the specific problems of postural weaknesses faced by riders.

Say hello to your spine

Your spine is an amazingly complex structure that functions like the internal foundation and framework of a building. It is supported by several groups of muscles in the upper and lower back. If your spine is not correctly aligned, then the postural muscles supporting it will also suffer. You will set up a cascade of compensatory motor patterns in which some muscles will become tighter and some weaker. The compensations go on to become habit and that's what makes them so hard to alter. Most of the time, you are oblivious to your muscular imbalances. They are simply the way you move.

1 Balance your spine

The first thing to focus on is balancing your spine so that it takes fewer forces to hold it up against gravity and then you can work on the deep muscles that support it. You have to discover how your spine tends to align itself. Most people fall into one of two categories: *swaybacks* and *slumpers*. One posture is not any worse than the other, it's just that each one tends to make certain muscles weaker and others tighter. Your alignment will be compromised further if you also have a slight *sideways curve* (scoliosis) in your spine. A scoliosis can be present in both a swayback and a slumper. All postural types have different problems while on the horse that fundamentally affect their riding efficiency.

2 Support your core

The next step is to learn to support your core. The main muscles that support the lower back form a kind of natural corset made up of several sets of interweaving muscles that work together to hold us upright. A well-supported core on the horse holds the body steady and allows the arms and legs to move independently, leading to that look of softness and stillness that is so apparent in naturally gifted riders. On the other hand, an unstable core affects riding in a host of ways. At best you will develop compensation patterns like gripping and tensing. At worst you will suffer from neck or back pain.

3 Stretch where you're tight

Improving stability and correcting common imbalances in the spine requires stretching tight areas to develop better range of movement. Using your body in a particular pattern all the time means that some important postural muscles lose flexibility. This tends to happen in two main areas: around the hips and legs and around the shoulders, upper back and neck. These tight spots not only contribute to poor alignment but also cause gripping and tightening on the horse. Loosening them up will allow you to create a straighter shoulder-hip-heel line, as well as making you feel freer and more comfortable in the saddle and in all aspects of your life.

4 Strengthen your limbs

Strong limbs contribute significantly to a stable, aligned body and allow you to take the load off your lower back and neck. Once you have rebalanced your spine, improved your core stability and stretched the parts of your body that are stiff, you can get to work on strengthening your arms and legs. The *Riding from the Inside Out* program contains strengthening exercises for targeting 'riding specific' muscle groups. The exercises are simple, yet very effective.

5 Gain muscle control

When you have an understanding of which muscles require strengthening, the next step is to achieve control over key muscles that affect how we ride. This means performing simple exercises designed to help your brain connect with the deep muscles that underpin larger muscle actions. The combination of building greater strength and power in these areas with an enhanced sense of control over them will make a striking difference to your riding.

To find out more about the Physiocise method, visit www.physiocise.com.au

6 Change your thinking

You can't fix your posture or stabilise your core on or off the horse until you are fully aware of any imbalances that you have and the ingrained patterns of movement you have developed in response. Another major principle of the Physiocise method is learning to pay attention to how you breathe, sit, stand, carry and walk throughout your day and not just to see the exercises as an aid to riding. As you gradually become more aware of your postural habits, you will be able to interrupt automatic, unconscious motor patterns and replace them with new ones that will strengthen your spine and allow your muscles to work better.

Unfortunately, habit is a powerful force. It takes a great deal of time to retrain your muscles so that they adopt new ways of moving. You will need plenty of gentle persistence and patience. Don't expect things to improve dramatically in a few weeks, but keep on reminding yourself of your postural cues and inevitably your body will begin to respond. This process of changing your awareness is crucial to long-term success and entails an on-going commitment.

getting started

Regardless of your riding discipline you've probably read books, watched videos and heard master trainers talk about perfect riding technique. The huge breakthrough that I received from learning about the Physiocise method was an understanding of the common compensation patterns that prevent riders from improving their technique. Recognise yourself in this?

breath-holding/ elevated shoulders	1	relaxed breathing
unstable seat	2	stable seat
overuse of legs	3	good leg control
rigid arms	4	soft arms
unsteady hands	5	steady, even hands
stiff joints	6	elastic joints that move with the horse

Riding from the Inside Out applies the key Physiocise principles to all of these patterns and provides exercises to rectify them. You have to work through each part in order, moving on to the next one as you begin to feel more familiar and confident with the exercises.

Each part is interrelated, however, and the full benefit of using Physiocise to fix your riding will be realised when you can apply all your newly learned skills together.

The exercises throughout have been developed specifically for riders and are guaranteed to improve your technique and change the way you ride. But because riding is such a complex activity that requires intense concentration, it makes sense to start to retrain your body off the horse. As you begin to notice changes in your body, you will be able to apply them while riding, but to start with it's better to learn new skills on terra firma.

You might think that the exercises seem surprisingly easy. None of them require a fitness background like mine or a high degree of ability. They have been devised so you can learn them on your own and perform them confidently at home. But they are deceptively powerful and effective, especially if you take the time to practise them regularly. You don't need hours and hours— just 20 minutes or so a day for a lifetime of better riding. It's an investment every bit as worthwhile as riding lessons.

On the bonus audio CD that comes with this book, Anna-Louise talks you through key exercises, giving you practice tips to help you perform each one correctly.

equipment

In the early stages, you need several simple pieces of equipment to act as visual cues to help your brain work out where you are in space. It's important to perform each exercise correctly or else you won't improve and the equipment I recommend will really help your form.

Posture dots

Anna-Louise developed the use of these handy little devices, which are invaluable in helping to prompt your brain to maintain your perfect posture. These packets of stick-on-dots, roughly 1.5cm in diameter, are available from newsagencies everywhere.

Bottom clencher

Another of Anna-Louise's innovations. The idea with this sophisticated piece of technology is to slip it between the cheeks of your buttocks to get those powerful muscles working strongly. A credit card works perfectly for this.

A chair

The best kind of chair is one that doesn't have arms or wheels. It should be firm and have an open but solid back.

A bar and a full-length mirror

These are used for your stretching exercises. The bar can be something like the railing of a balcony or anything that won't fall over when you pull on it. The mirror is helpful when you first start so you can see how you're moving during an exercise. How you think you look and what you really look like are often two completely different things.

A fitball

Some exercises designed to be performed on a chair can also be performed on a fitball if you have one. Anti-burst balls are available from all good sporting stores. They come in various sizes and it's important to select the right size for your height and weight. If it's wrong, your ball could contribute to poor alignment. If you are up to 155 cm tall, use a 55 cm ball. If you are between 155 cm and 175 cm, use a 65 cm ball. If you are taller than 175 cm, use a 75 cm ball.

An exercise band

This is an elasticised band about 1.5 m in length that is used for some exercises. You may be able to obtain one from local sporting and fitness stores, or from fitness websites.

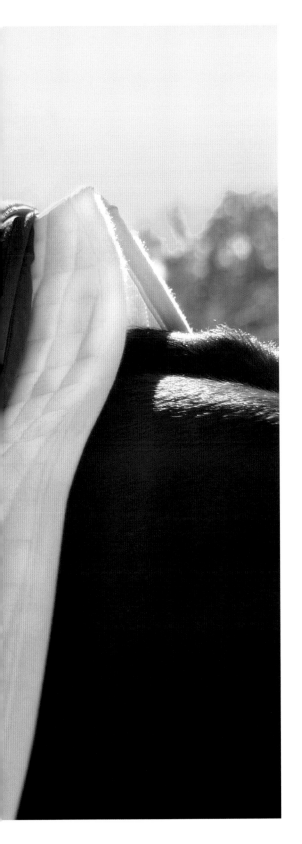

part one

Balanced riding

the foundation of good riding

Good posture is the key to good riding. In fact, posture is an essential, if often overlooked, element of good health in general. It is a way of doing things with more energy, less strain and less muscle fatigue. With good posture:

- the bones are properly aligned
- your muscles, joints and ligaments can work as they're supposed to.

Because poor posture can affect many important bodily systems, such as digestion, elimination, breathing and the movement of muscles, joints and ligaments, it is important for our lifelong health to maintain dynamic, stable posture.

Unfortunately, 21st century living has given most of us 21st century bodies. We sit more than ever before at work and at leisure, we drive more and more and it is difficult to find ways to make incidental physical activity a general part of everyday life. As a result, many of us have weakened postural muscles supporting the spine and find it difficult to sit or stand straight for any length of time.

Healthy and stable

The spine has four main sections: two loading and two moving. The loading ones are:

1 the thoracic spine (with the ribcage that wraps around from front to back)
2 the pelvis (which helps to maintain the base of the spine).

Because they have many bones joining them from the front and sides, they also generally have limited movement and are inherently more stable.

The moving sections are the neck and the lower back. They do not have many bones around them to provide structural support, which gives them great freedom of movement. They can twist, bend, turn and straighten. Instead they rely on muscular corsets for support.

If your spine is misaligned then you may develop an unconscious compensatory pattern to try to overcome it. The source of these can be divided into two basic types:

1 *structural imbalances* are physical characteristics with which you're born, such as having one leg longer than the other or a scoliosis
2 *muscular imbalances* are characteristics such as poor core stability or tight muscles and are often a result of the body trying to compensate for sloppy posture, old injuries or structural problems.

In perfect standing posture all the sections of the spine are balanced and the muscle corsets are strong enough to assist in maintaining alignment through a full range of movement. There is an absence of compensatory patterns or they are efficiently controlled. The well-balanced spine takes fewer forces to hold it upright and movement has a smooth and fluid quality as there is less strain being carried in the body.

Give yourself a good long look in the mirror and check out your own alignment. The first thing you have to establish is whether you are a swayback or a slumper and whether or not you also have a sideways curve. I was amazed to discover when I began to work with Anna-Louise that I have a slight sideways curve in my right side with a bit of a swayback to boot.

what type are you?

1 Are you a swayback?

- Does your tummy have a tendency to pop out?
- Do your feet tend to turn out?
- Do you have tight muscles at the front of your hips?
- Do you have tight calf muscles?
- Are you generally flexible with the exception of your hips and calves?

2 Are you a slumper?

- Are you stiff between your shoulder blades?
- Are you tight in your hamstrings?
- Does your tummy have a tendency to spread?
- Does your breathing tend to be shallow?
- Do your hips tend to sit in front of your body?

what type are you?

3 Are you a sideways curver?

It's a bit trickier to work out if you have a sideways curve. Follow these steps to see if you have a structural sideways curve in your spine.

- Stand in front of the mirror, preferably without a top on, with both feet parallel and 30 cm apart.
- Lift your chest slightly and then check to see if your shoulders are level. You may see immediately that one shoulder is lower than the other.
- Now look at your waist on the side of the lower shoulder. You will probably notice that you are more dropped on this side and the angle of your waist is more acute. This is due to the slight sideways bend in your spine.
- You have to become aware that you tend to drop to that side in order to straighten yourself up again.

Here is **another way** to identify on which side you tend to **curve.**

Stand with your weight first on one leg and then the other. It's likely you will be able to tell straight away which side you prefer. If standing with your left leg straight and your right leg bent feels the most comfortable to you, you are a right sideways curver.

Remember that many people will either sway or slump, and then have a bit of a sideways curve for good measure!

standing tall

M ost of us have a combination of subtle structural and muscular imbalances that present their unique challenges to overcome. Fortunately, the human body is surprisingly malleable and new habits can be instituted that result in permanent change. You just need to keep at it.

One of the easiest and most effective new things you can do is to become aware of how you stand. Most of us tend to stand with weight on one leg and our feet rotated out at various angles. This puts uneven pressure on the spine and can switch off the deep stabilising muscles that hold up the moving part of the lower back. The sloppier the stance, the harder for muscles to hold you upright. Even worse is constantly leaning against things such as walls or counters rather than standing up unaided, as this makes lazy muscles even weaker and less capable of providing support.

When standing, focus on balancing from the ground up. Keep your feet parallel and your weight distributed evenly between them as this makes it easier for the rest of the spine to maintain alignment.

Think of aligning your body on 'traintracks' with your feet, knees, hips and shoulders all in line with one another.

Naturally you'll find yourself slipping back into sloppy patterns, but the more you remind yourself to balance your spine when standing the more you'll retrain your muscles to hold you upright.

the slumper in action

The slumper tends to sit with the chest collapsing in, the upper back rounded, the tummy spreading and the bottoms bones rolled forward. The head may also protrude forward. The slumper's problems are more likely to be muscular than structural.

When a **slumper** is riding
you might see

- Incorrect arm angle—the hands can drop too low and/or the arms can become too straight.
- Elbows may tend to stick out.
- Feet will move backwards to compensate for the forward slump.
- Thigh or knee may grip to compensate for the lack of balance.

- Head will tend to be dropped with the eyes looking down.
- Feet will be unstable in the stirrups.
- Forward movement of the horse may be suppressed because the bottom bones are 'out the front door'.
- Horse may tend to be on the forehand, reflecting the rider's slump.

the swayback in action

From the waist up, the swayback tends to have good posture. The problems begin lower down as they have an increase in curvature in the lower back and their problems have a structural basis. Typically, they sit with their bottoms sticking out and their stomachs popping out at the front. They tend to be tight through the hips and calves and their feet tend to rotate outwards.

When a **swayback** is riding
you might see

- Chin may be up with head tilted slightly back.
- Hands may be unstable.
- Stiffness through the elbows.
- A very rigid look.
- Lack of movement in the hip joint due to tight hip flexors (particularly apparent in the rising trot where the whole body tends to rise as a unit, rather than an opening and closing action happening in the hip).
- Bouncing out of the saddle.
- Knees may grip.
- Toes will be rotated outwards.
- Difficulty keeping the stirrups on the balls of the feet.
- Suppressed movement of horse because the bottom bones are 'out the back door'.
- Horse hollows, a reflection of the rider's swayback.

the sideways curver in action

Sideways curving (scoliosis) is surprisingly widespread. *Structural scoliosis* usually affects the bones in the thoracic spine, between the shoulder blades. If the position of the vertebrae changes, a muscle imbalance develops to compensate.

Postural scoliosis can occur as a result of doing something too often on one side, such as always carrying something heavy on one shoulder or having to constantly bend or twist to one side. Standing with the weight more on one leg than the other may be another reason for sideways unevenness. In these cases, it's the muscle imbalance that creates the curve in the spine. Postural scoliosis is much more common than structural scoliosis. The biggest problem with sideways curving, no matter its origin, is that it makes the muscles on one side slightly tighter than the other.

When a **sideways curver** is riding you might see

- Tilting to one side in the saddle.
- One hip 'collapsed'.
- Head may tilt to one side.
- Hands may become unlevel (the 'driving the car around a corner' look).
- May find riding on one rein easier than the other.
- May put a spur mark on one side only (the leg will grip on the opposite side to the curve to hang on, or will dig in on the same side of the curve).
- Difficulty keeping the stirrups on the ball of the foot.
- May lose one stirrup more than the other.
- Body may have a tendency to twist.
- Horse may tend to over-bend, a reflection of the rider's sideways curve.

more good looks

There are really only three incorrect postural patterns—swayback, slumping and sideways curving. The body is very clever at working out ways to compensate for your postural imbalances. You may not have the classic slumping, swaying or sideways curve presentation when you ride, but you may lean forward, lean back or become twisted.

The photos opposite all show further compensation patterns in the saddle. Often, a slumper will try to sit up straight by leaning backwards. Riders with a swayback may try to bring their shoulders forward by leaning forward. Or, sideways curvers who have ineffective leg aids may twist their whole body to try to make the horse bend or go sideways. The photos make it clear what happens to our alignment on the horse when these compensation patterns kick in.

It's important to take a close look at your own postural and riding habits—it's guaranteed that there is a link between the two.

How our **riding posture** influences **our horses**

While doing the photographs for this book, it became increasingly apparent that the horse mimics the incorrect postural pattern of the rider. When Larissa slumped, the horse went on the forehand. When she arched too far into a swayback, the horse hollowed through its back and shortened in the neck. If she curved excessively to one side it showed up as over-bend in the horse (to the side of the curve) and a falling out of the shoulder to the stiffer side.

Larissa also had made some interesting comments as she rode around in the incorrect positions. As she did circle after circle slumping, while we tried to capture just the right image, she called out, 'I can't breathe like this!' When she had to ride for a while with a swayback, she said, 'My feet are swinging all over the place.' And when it came time to shoot the correct positions, she breathed a sigh of relief, found her balance, the horse carried himself much better and harmony was restored!

Leaning forward

- May be a swayback trying to bring their shoulders forward but can happen with a slumper as well.
- Can be a fear response (when riding unruly or young horses).
- Legs come back, heels tend to go up.
- Hands are often locked down, balancing on the reins.
- Head tilts down and the eyes look down.
- Bottom is out.
- Horse goes on the forehand.

Leaning back

- May be a slumper who is trying to sit more upright.
- Feet and legs go forward.
- Arms become too straight, balancing on reins.
- Creates inability to release rein contact effectively.
- Shows a tendency to 'water-ski' off the horse's head.
- Can make the horse 'tuck-in' and become tight over the poll.

Twisted

- Usually occurs in sideways curvers.
- Results from ineffectiveness in seat and legs, so the rider twists to try to put horse in correct shape.
- One hip may be collapsed.
- One leg may become shorter and grip more than the other.
- Hands will be uneven.
- Hands and arms lose alignment with the horse.

balance your bottom bones

To find your correct alignment for sitting, you have to learn how to balance your bottom bones and lift your dots. This is an extremely useful exercise that could change the way you sit forever, both on and off the horse.

What to do

- Sit on the edge of the chair with your feet parallel and about riding distance apart.

- Find your bottom bones by placing your hands under your buttocks and feeling for the two hard bones.

- Now do the best slump you can. Feel how your bottom bones moved in front of your fingertips? This is called letting your bottom bones go 'out the front door'. Notice how your chest drops and your stomach spreads.

- Now gently roll your bottom bones back and overarch your spine. Feel how your bottom bones moved behind your fingertips? They've now gone 'out the back door'.

- Slump and overarch several times to familiarise yourself with each position.

- Now find the middle point between the two. Take your hands out and, voilà! In this position your bottom bones are balanced and so is your spine.

- Finally, lift your centre dot, trying to make the distance between your centre dot and your belly button greater without changing the position of your spine. Keep your head poised above your balanced spine.

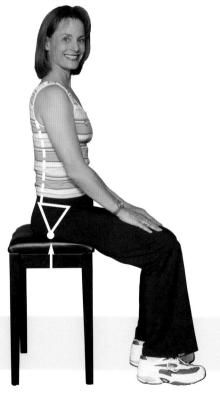

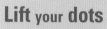

Lift your dots

You will benefit from wearing posture dots for most of the exercises in *Riding from the Inside Out* as they give you an excellent sense of your upper body alignment. Put one dot on each shoulder on the boney bit you can feel at the front. Stick a third dot on at the end of your sternum, or breastbone, just before it starts to dip into your chest. This creates a dot triangle. If you don't have posture dots, just imagine this triangle.

When your **bottom bones** are **balanced** on the horse you will see

- The shoulder/hip/heel line will be perpendicular to the ground.
- Head will follow the natural curvature of the spine, not tilting down or up.
- Chest will be open.
- Shoulders will be level.
- Elbows will be close to the sides.
- Elbow-wrist-bit line will be straight.
- Hands will be level.
- Arms and legs will move softly around a stable core.
- No gripping with the knees and thighs.
- Balls of the feet will sit balanced on the stirrups.
- Toes will face forward.
- Lower leg will be still.
- Body will absorb and move with the movement of the horse.
- Aids will be more subtle.
- Carriage will remain still.
- All of these elements also apply when riding in the forward seat with the exception that the perpendicular line becomes shoulder-knee-toe.

core stability

Now that you are beginning to understand how to balance your spine, you must learn how to keep it balanced. To do this, you need to develop your core stability. This is the ability of your deep postural muscles to act-ively support your spine in all of your movement patterns.

Gifted riders have incredible innate core stability (often without being aware of it) that allows their arms and legs to function independently and leads to that wonderful sense of effortless softness and stillness they exhibit when they ride. These individuals comprise only the smallest number of riders, however; most of us have to improve stability in our midsection through specific exercises.

Stabilising something is very different from making it stronger. I had been aware of the importance of core *strength* for years and had been exercising on a fitball and other unstable devices. However, I was shocked to discover that, because of my muscle strength, I was turning on all the wrong muscles instead of my deep core. Stability is being able to maintain alignment for long periods without fatigue. I didn't know it, but my sideways curve and swayback had tipped me so out of balance that I couldn't sit in a chair for any length of time without slumping, let alone stay upright and in control on a horse.

Two types of muscle

The body has two main groups of muscle: *postural* and *global*.

Postural muscles hold us in place. They are composed of slow-twitch muscle fibres that stay on for a long time at a low grade without getting tired. All our deep, stabilising muscles are of the postural type and they are working away most of the time, even though we're usually not conscious of their activity.

Global muscles are generally bigger, stronger muscle groups on the outer surface of the body that we use for movement and power. They are composed of fast-twitch muscle fibres that can be recruited effectively in bursts but tire easily and have to switch off again.

When the postural muscles of the core are weak and underdeveloped, the surrounding global muscle groups happily kick in to help hold us upright. But because they are not designed for this function, they often fatigue as they work to compensate for the inefficiency of the deeper postural muscles. The more challenging the physical activity—such as horse-riding—the more the global muscles are called upon.

Signs that the global muscles are overworking on the horse are such things as gripping, tilting and tension and the need to constantly push and pull. Riding exaggerates the inadequacies of core stability because of the dynamic movement of the horse. The rider then overcompensates with the global muscles, which is a lot of hard work that unfortunately never produces beautiful and balanced riding.

Our hidden muscles

One of the reasons why it's hard to recognise that your problems could be caused by poor alignment and an unstable core is that postural muscles lie deep within the torso and can't be felt in the same way that you know your quads or your biceps are working. Because we can't see them and they work very subtly, we have to treat them differently to our big, outer muscles. Two things can help you improve your core stability:

1 an increased awareness of your alignment

2 exercises to gradually retrain the muscles to function fully

Changing your awareness of your alignment is an on-going process to overcome old habits and replace them with new ones.

To exercise the deep corset, you have to first understand exactly which muscles are involved. The deep corset has three main parts. It has

1 a lid, which is the diaphragm

2 walls made up of the deepest abdominal muscles, the transversus abdominus and the multifidus muscle of the back

3 a floor, better known as the pelvic floor muscles.

These muscles are all very closely related. When they work well they control and maintain the balanced position of your spine and help you maintain beautiful posture on and off the horse.

The exercises in this section provide splendid assistance in improving awareness and exercising the deep corset. They can kick-start your new approach by giving you the opportunity to concentrate on how your core functions and they will also strengthen those difficult-to-reach muscles. To start with, set time aside every day to work on your core. As your endurance improves, you'll start to feel more balanced in the saddle. And that will feel very satisfying.

The deep corset

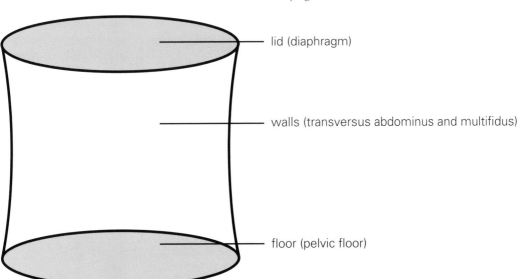

lid (diaphragm)

walls (transversus abdominus and multifidus)

floor (pelvic floor)

the lid of the corset

The lid of the corset is formed by the diaphragm at the base of the lungs. It moves up and down as you breathe in and out. It allows you to breathe and keep your postural muscles working at the same time when it functions efficiently as part of the corset. Once you have good control over it, you can use its assistance to activate the walls and the floor. You will also be able to release the strain in your upper back, shoulders and arms.

You may be surprised to learn that breathing well is the first step to developing a stable core. In our frantic, time-poor lives, many of us have developed inadequate breathing habits and our breath gets stuck in the top one-third of the chest. This can become very tiring as shallow breathing brings on unnecessary tension in the neck and shoulders. Furthermore, it means that air can seep into the stomach, inhibiting full activation of the corset and leading to that annoying little pot belly that plagues some of us.

Breathing well on the horse
Breathing well benefits riders not only because it plays a part in core stability. It also does much to relax tension throughout the body, especially the tightness in our necks and shoulders that is uncomfortable and cramps our posture. A neck that is free of tension allows the back to lengthen and widen, the shoulders to soften and the head to become more poised. This carriage looks graceful on the horse but it's also vital for good technique. And it reflects how we would like our horses to carry themselves. Tension blocks mobility in the shoulders, tightens rein contact and leads to harsh hands. As we are all aware, this confines the horse's neck and inhibits his strides. When this happens, you cannot hope to connect well with your horse.

The lungs and diaphragm comprise a complete physiological system, but they can only work together when we breathe deeply. If we take shallow breaths, the diaphragm moves less and so does the adjoining musculature in the rest of the corset.

When we inhale
- the lungs expand sideways as air is drawn into the lower parts
- the diaphragm drops down
- the pelvic floor relaxes slightly.

When we exhale
- the lungs constrict
- the diaphragm moves up
- the deep abdominal muscles contract
- the pelvic floor lifts up.

Have a look at yourself while you're breathing to see what you're doing.
- Sit on the edge of a chair in front of a mirror. Allow your body to slump.
- Take a few deep breaths in this position.
- Watch your neck and shoulders carefully. Are your shoulders moving? Are the muscles at the front of your neck obviously tense? If so, you're probably only using the upper parts of your lungs, your neck and your shoulder muscles while you breathe and you are not activating your diaphragm effectively.

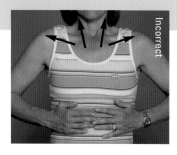

Incorrect

breathing 101

When you breathe the object is to get air into your system as efficiently as possible.
Start breathing better by learning to use the whole of your lungs, not just the upper portion.
To practise, try this breathing exercise.

What to do

- Sit on the edge of your chair. Balance your bottom bones and lift your dots.
- Place your hands gently on either side of your rib cage.
- Relax your neck and shoulders.
- Take a slow deep breath in to the count of 4.
- Breathe out slowly to the count of 4.

Focus

Imagine that your ribcage is gently pushing your hands sideways. It might help also to imagine that you are allowing your back to open and your breath is filling up your back. Use your hands to give you feedback about how the ribcage is expanding with each inhalation. Make sure you keep your neck and shoulders relaxed. Try not to force the deeper breath.

Good **breathing** technique

Anna-Louise generally recommends that you breathe in and out through your nose. If you find this difficult, breathe in through your nose and out through your mouth. When you are familiar with the exercises, you may want to play around with which breathing pattern allows you to achieve the greatest activation of your core. When you have practised these breathing exercises in a controlled way, think of your breathing regularly throughout your normal day. Balancing your bottom bones when you sit is an effective way to improve your alignment in your lower back and deep breathing will help to stabilise your core. When you get on the horse, you can practise breathing as part of your warm-up. The goal is to make the deeper breathing pattern automatic. You'll find that you carry much less tension in the saddle and that your seat improves too when you can do this.

the walls of the corset

The deep abdominal muscles form the walls of the corset. They interweave with the deep muscles around the spine, the multifidus, and are designed to work with them as a functional unit. Importantly, these muscles don't just play a part in our posture: they are also involved in joint stability, they hold our organs in place, they provide respiratory support and support of the circulatory and immune systems. They are essential to our complete well-being and are worth taking care of with consistent exercise.

Layer upon layer

The muscles of the abdominal complex are arranged in layers. Each one serves a different purpose as either a *mover* or a *stabiliser* and is composed of different muscle fibres according to function.

Having impressive muscle definition in this region is something most of us would like and some of us expend lots of energy trying to achieve. However, there's much more to a stable core than ripped abs and performing hundreds of crunches will not condition the deep muscle structures that provide vital support. If you're looking for better riding technique you are better off ditching traditional abdominal training, as I found out.

The wall of muscle in the abdominal complex is only about 1 cm thick. You may think that you have much more than that, but that could be because this area is also highly receptive to fat deposits. You will only notice your abdominal muscles if you are very lean.

The first layer of muscle runs vertically from just under the sternum to the pubic bone. This is the rectus abdominis, the muscle that develops into the famous six-pack when extensively trained. It is composed of fast-twitch fibres, so even though it can be switched on for intense work it fatigues quickly. Its function is to provide movement in the torso, not stability.

The next layer is a set of muscles on each side of the body called the external and internal obliques. The external obliques are the largest of your abdominal muscles. They run along the front and both sides of the trunk from the lower eight ribs, and insert into the crest of your pelvis. The internal obliques are located just under their partners and mimic their function. Both types are able to be recruited as stabilisers for certain activities, unlike rectus abdominis. But, once again, they are composed mainly of fast-twitch fibres and are useful for twisting and turning, not holding us upright in the saddle.

The deepest layer of abdominal muscle is the most important for better riding. This muscle is called the transversus abdominis (TA). It contains the most slow-twitch fibres and is the primary stabiliser of the abdominal complex. It is the only layer to wrap horizontally around the spine to work with the deep muscles of the lower back. When the corset is activated, TA and multifidus work in unison.

TA 101

TA is a muscle that is difficult to notice in the ordinary course of events. Eventually you will be able to recruit this all-important muscle automatically, but to begin you have to focus on very subtle sensations and learn how they feel. Don't expect anything too dramatic to begin with. Start practising in front of a mirror and soon you'll be able to do it without visual aids.

Equipment
- a chair
- a mirror

What to do
- Sit on the edge of the chair with your feet about riding distance apart.
- Balance your bottom bones and lift your dots.
- Place one hand on your ribcage and one hand on your lower abdomen. Allow it to fully sag out.
- Relax your neck and shoulders.
- Breathe in deeply and slowly through your nose to a count of 4, drawing the air into the lower part of your lungs and keeping your shoulders relaxed.
- Breathe out slowly to a count of 4 while visualising your abdomen moving in gently towards your spine.
- Repeat this cycle of allowing the abdomen to sag while you inhale and drawing in gently while you exhale.

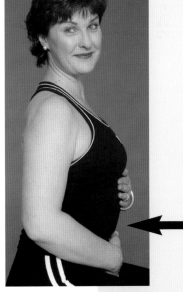

Focus
Keep your body stable while you gently activate your TA. Make sure you don't over-breathe and tense your diaphragm because if you fill your stomach with too much air your corset will switch off. It's important not to 'suck' your tummy in. The movement is very subtle. With practice, your TA will stay activated even when you're not thinking about it.

the base of the corset

The base of the corset is made up of a sling of slow-twitch muscles, also arranged in layers, called the pelvic floor. These muscles run from the pubic bones at the front of the pelvis through to the coccyx at the back and support all the organs in this area in both the male and female body. The pelvic floor muscles move up and down subtly as you breathe in and out, a little like a trampoline. When they are activated, they help to fire TA and vice versa. Once you are able to link an activated pelvic floor with good breathing technique, you will be able to stabilise your core with a strong, supportive base.

Secret business

To exercise the pelvic floor muscles, you need to picture a point in the centre of the sling. You are about to learn some interesting tips for activating your pelvic floor muscles, but don't be put off!

For women that centre point of the sling is the vagina. A good cue is to imagine a straw coming out of your vagina that has a small pea on the end of it. Breathe in and as you breathe out imagine you are drawing the pea up into the straw without squeezing your buttocks.

For men the centre of the sling is the testicles. Your cue is to imagine your testicles are sitting firmly in contact with a saddle. As you breathe out, imagine you are lifting your crown jewels just gently off the saddle without changing the position of your spine.

What you are aiming for is a deep, drawing-in feeling as you exhale. Eventually this will become habit and you won't notice it, but to start with you'll probably find yourself letting go completely as you breathe in and switching on completely as you breathe out. Gradually this will establish itself as a partial releasing and contracting as you breathe that you will be able to maintain comfortably because the muscles are composed of slow-twitch fibres designed to fire at a low grade for long periods.

Say **hello** to your
pelvic floor

Still need help finding your pelvic floor? Try putting your thumb into the roof of your mouth and pressing it strongly against your upper palette. As you do this, suck as hard as you can on your thumb. For some people, this action triggers an unmistakable contraction in the pelvic floor.

The rider's pelvic floor

One hint that you may be weak at the base of your core is that you use global compensatory muscles, such as the adductors in your inner thighs, when you are riding. This will manifest itself in tenseness in the legs and a tendency to grip with the inside of the legs rather than being able to keep them free from tension. You have to strengthen your pelvic floor without squeezing the gluteals (the large muscles in your bottom) or the adductors, otherwise you are just relying on your compensatory patterns again. It may help to begin with to practise the pelvic floor exercises with your eyes closed so you can focus fully on the correct technique. As you grow more accustomed to what you're trying to achieve, keep your eyes open so you can take note of your surroundings while still remaining conscious of your core—more like you'll have to do when you're riding.

It takes lots of time and practice to retrain deep postural muscles and you may find it's 10 weeks or more before you begin to notice improvements on or off the horse. You know how difficult it can be to develop good control in certain riding skills. Approach training the pelvic floor—and therefore the deep corset—in the same way.

Wondering how your core stability stacks up?

Try this simple test.

- Sit on the edge of your chair with your feet riding distance apart. They should be directly under your knees.

- Balance your bottom bones and lift your dots.

- Place your hands on your hips with your fingertips just in front of the boney bits you can feel.

- Now, slowly and gently lift your right foot a few centimetres off the floor.

- Notice if your body is compensating in any way. Did you lean to the side? Did your hip position change? Did you feel your upper body move?

- Now try it on the other side. What did you notice this time? Was it harder or easier than the first side? Did you notice your body compensating to perform the lift?

pelvic floor 101

Try isolating the pelvic floor while lying down to start with. When you feel more sure of the action, try it while standing or sitting on the edge of a chair on balanced bottom bones. Then you can gradually increase your control through a range of movement.

What to do

- Lie on your back with your feet on the floor and your knees bent.

- Set yourself up on train tracks with your feet, knees, hips and shoulders in line with one another.

- Find the balanced position of your spine. Gently flatten your back as far as it will go, then arch as far as it will go. Now find the middle of those two positions. If you slip one hand under your back you will find that there is a little space under your back.

- Place one hand on your ribcage and one hand on your lower abdomen.

- Breathe in deeply through the nose to a slow count of 4 and imagine relaxing the pelvic floor muscles.

- Breathe out to a count of 4 and visualise drawing the pea up the straw or lifting the jewels off the saddle. Feel your abdomen soften and lower towards your spine.

- Repeat 8 to 10 times.

Focus

Make sure you are not carrying any tension in any other part of your body, such as the back of your neck or your jaw, while you concentrate on linking your breathing with the soft drawing-in movement in your pelvic floor.

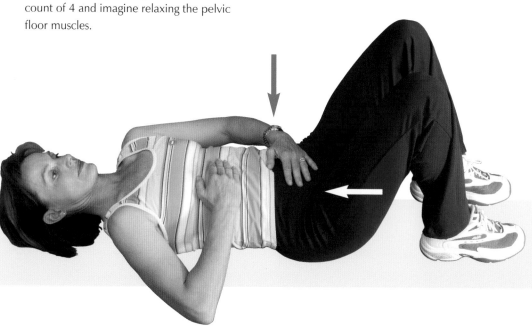

standing pelvic floor

Equipment
- a kitchen bench, balcony railing, or back of a chair

What to do
- Start about 1 m behind your chair with your hands resting on the back.
- Stand with your bottom slightly out, your feet less than hip-width apart and your toes pointing slightly inward.
- Keep your knees straight. Relax your neck and shoulders. Let your abdomen relax, but watch out for letting your back sway.
- Breathe in deeply to a slow count of 4 and breathe out to a count of 4 while drawing the pea up the straw or the jewels off the saddle.

- The abdominal wall will activate as you draw in your pelvic floor on the exhalation.
- Repeat 8 to 10 times.

Focus
Keep your legs apart to prevent you from relying on your strong inner thigh muscles to cheat. Try not to squeeze your buttocks. Don't try too hard. Soften your breath and relax your upper body. Start with 8 to 10 breaths and build up to maintaining the rhythm for longer stretches.

leg in leg out

The added leg movement in this exercise will challenge your core stability. Keeping your core stable while the leg is moving simulates what has to happen on the horse. Your leg needs to move independently around a stable base. This is the perfect way to practice.

What to do

- Lie on your back with your knees bent up.
- Set yourself up on train tracks.
- Establish your balanced spine position. Arch too far, press your back into the mat, then find the middle.
- Place your left hand under the small of your back and your right hand on your tummy just below your belly button.
- Breathe in slowly to a count of 4.
- As you slowly breathe out, let the left leg open slightly while you think of drawing up your pelvic floor muscles.
- Breathe in and return the leg to the starting position.
- Repeat 10 times on each side.
- Increase the number of repetitions up to 30 as you build control.

Focus

Make sure to use the out breath to activate your core, which in turn stabilises the pelvis. Allow your knee to drop and return to centre with the rhythm of your breathing and keep the movement smooth and continuous. Focus all the time on the image of drawing up the pelvic floor muscles into the body. It takes strong visual imagery to get the breathing and muscle activation coordinated.

The hand under your back will help you check that your spine remains stable. When you begin to feel pressure on your hand it means your pelvis is rolling and you've gone too far. If your shoulder is aching, just remove your hand from behind your back and place it on your abdomen. Use the hand on your abdo-men for feedback on whether your deep corset is activating. You will feel your hand dropping towards your spine if it is activating correctly. If the abdomen pushes up and out against your hand, you are trying too hard and probably holding your breath.

Incorrect

Deep **breath** out

We have designed these exercises that recruit the pelvic floor to activate the entire deep corset for a number of reasons. The main one is that if you merely focus on 'sucking your tummy in' (that is, just activating the walls) you are more likely to use the superficial abdominal layers rather than the deeper ones of the corset. When using the pelvic floor you will find that the drawing-in feeling is slow and controlled and it is harder to cheat by recruiting your global muscles. The great Australian research of Hodges and O'Sullivan and colleagues (see the References on page 111) has found that the pelvic floor gently lifts as the breath goes out. So while it might feel a bit odd to start with, stick with activating your corset from the floor for more lasting results.

virtual reality

This exercise helps further to open up motor pathways to your deep corset. It's similar to the stability test on page 39. It's called 'Virtual reality' because you only visualise the movement of your leg.

Equipment
- a chair

What to do
- Sit on the edge of the chair with your feet about riding distance apart.
- Balance your bottom bones and lift your dots.
- Place your fingers on your hip bones so you can feel if you move excessively.
- Breathe in through your nose to a count of 4, opening the ribcage and drawing the air into the lower part of your lungs.
- Breathe out to a count of 4 and visualise drawing your pelvic floor muscles up into your body. At the same time, visualise lifting your right foot off the floor without letting it leave the ground.
- The drawing-up of your pelvic floor muscles should cause TA to move away from your fingertips. This is a sure sign that it is firing.
- Repeat 5 times on each side.

Focus
Use the activation of your deep corset to keep your body as stable as possible as you visualise the movement. Try to avoid leaning to the side or backwards. Keep the shoulders still and the neck relaxed. Maintain the balanced sitting position and avoid slumping or overarching the lower back.

Incorrect

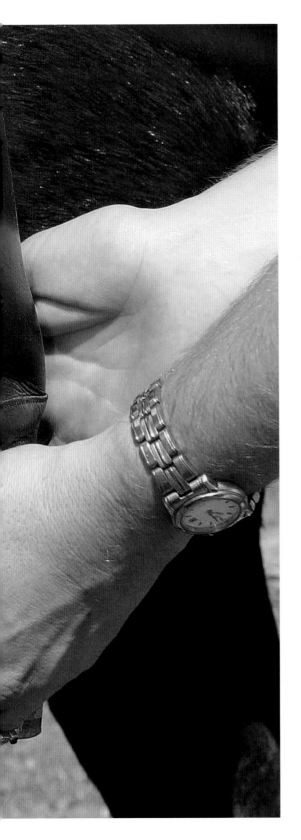

part two

Grounded
riding

legs behaving badly

As I continued to retrain my alignment and stabilise my core with the Physiocise method, my heightened body awareness made me ever more conscious that my legs and feet were just not cooperating when I was on the horse. The most annoying and constant reminder of this was that I kept losing my stirrups, especially in the sitting trot. I could feel both feet wobbling, but I was especially aware of my right foot swinging backwards and forwards. No matter how hard I tried (one of my fatal flaws as it just introduces more strain in my body) I could not keep my feet still. Thinking laterally, Larissa tried tying my right stirrup to the girth to stabilise my foot. It definitely did the trick, but I couldn't believe how tired my leg felt. Obviously this strategy was forcing me to use a whole new series of muscles. We both realised that, while effective in the short term, it didn't address why I had the problem in the first place.

A few lessons later I was cantering around on the left rein and suddenly realised that my right knee and foot were pointing outwards. I remember stopping halfway around the circle and saying to Larissa, 'How come my right foot is pointing to the outside when I'm on the left rein? It feels all wrong!' Then, a short while later, we were working on some shoulder-in on the circle and I could not get my leg to connect with the horse in a way that helped him be in the right shape. Larissa showed me how her leg worked and it was then that we noticed that I didn't have the ability to use my lower leg without bending my knee and raising my heel.

We could clearly see (and I could feel) the problems, but neither of us knew how to fix them. I was experiencing the same frustrations over and over again. Intellectually I could understand what Larissa wanted me to do, but I couldn't connect those messages from my brain to my muscles in order to activate the right movement patterns.

From watching the riding style of Larissa and other talented riders I had a clear mental imprint of what classically correct and balanced riding looks like. So Anna-Louise and I analysed this ideal in comparison to my own riding. What I began to understand was that, because I lacked deep core stability in my trunk and flexibility in my hips, I was using other muscles to compensate. The problem with my riding was not just faulty technique, it went deeper than that. I couldn't achieve the riding ideal I yearned for because I physically lacked the stability and flexibility to do so. Add to this years of compensating for my postural imbalances and I really had a lot of layers to peel back.

After a thorough assessment, Anna-Louise worked out that the reason my right foot kept swinging was because of chronic ligament tightness in my right hip. This was causing the whole leg to sit rotated, and consequently the foot wobbled, moved exessively fowards and backwards and I kept losing the stirrup. My unconscious compensation was to grip through my thigh in an attempt to keep my leg in and the foot still. Unfortunately, the tightness in my hip was overriding all my good intentions and the foot rotated and wobbled, no matter how hard I tried. This is a classic example of a compensatory pattern inhibiting good riding technique.

The key to developing **truly grounded riding** is a combination of:

1 stretching
2 strengthening
3 gaining control

In order to undo this pattern and learn to use my leg as a whole, I had to maintain the work of improving my alignment and developing deep core strength. I also had to get to work on my lower body, specifically around my pelvis as this is the part of the body which most influences good alignment. This entailed stretching the tight ligaments in my right hip, strengthening the muscles in my lower body and then learning to control the essential 'riding specific' hip muscles.

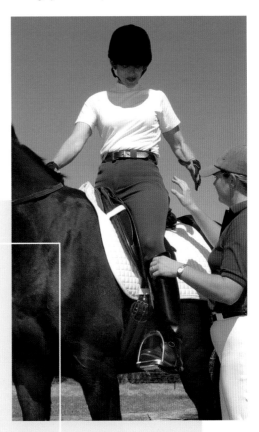

the hip and leg muscles

Many of the major muscle groups in the lower body are strong and active global muscles. Ideally, the deeper postural muscles stabilise the trunk and pelvis and the larger, global muscles come in to play when we have to move that stable unit, such as when we walk. But, as we've seen, if postural muscles are weak the global muscle system will attempt to compensate. This leads to imbalance, strain and chronic tightness and weakness. By stretching out your legs and hips you can alleviate some of that tightness, which in turn helps you to rebalance your spine. With less resistance from tight ligaments it should be easier to maintain your alignment and you can work on stabilising your deep corset around this balanced spine.

The hips are the strongest joints in your body and they support all your weight when you are upright. Their rotational ability allows you to move the lower part of your torso through a wide range of motion. The hip, groin and leg muscles are attached either to your spine or your pelvis (or sometimes both) so they affect the alignment of the spine. The lower back is often called upon to compensate for tightness in the hip, leg and groin area. Tight muscles that are never stretched can pull the spine into a too swayed or too slumped posture. Unfortunately, sitting all day with poor posture increases shortness and tightness, which is the reason why so many of us have reduced flexibility in this key area.

There are five major muscle groups to familiarise yourself with.

The psoas muscles

These large hip flexor muscles originate in your back, cross through the abdomen and finish in the groin. They are reasonably thick in diameter: each one is about the size of a good pork fillet. Consequently, when they are very tight they can increase a swayback by pulling on the lumbar vertebrae from the front. If you have a marked swayback, you may find that stretching the psoas allows for easier activation of your core because the spine is in a more relaxed position.

Even if you are a slumper, you may find that these muscles can still be tight depending on how you use your hips when you ride. So try the psoas stretches and see how much better you feel in the saddle.

The gluteal muscles

Like many other hard-working muscles, the glutes are composed of layers. Generally when we consider our buttocks we are referring to the big one we can see, the gluteus maximus, but there are some other deeper gluteal muscles that play an important role in pelvic stability. These are the gluteus medius and the gluteus minimus.

The hamstring muscles

The hamstrings are a group of muscles running from the pelvis to the back of the knee. If they're inflexible they can affect the alignment of the spine through their attachment to the pelvis. The tighter they are, the more they pull you into a slumped posture—although if you are a slumper to begin with, then you'll develop really tight hamstrings. It's hard to know which comes first.

If you are having trouble balancing yourself in the saddle or activating your gluteal muscles in particular, your problem may be tight hamstrings. Try bending forward next to a mirror. Can you get near your toes or are the tips of your fingers barely reaching your shins? If it's the latter, you have to get stretching. It will not only improve your riding but all your movements.

The adductors

The adductors (or groin muscles) are strong muscles in the inner thigh. They also attach to the pelvis, starting just below your pubic bone and extending down the inside of both legs to just above your knee. Any rider knows that they are critical to stable riding. However, because they are strong, global muscles they are frequently recruited to compensate for poor core stability. When they are over-used in the saddle, you see thigh or knee gripping and poor alignment. Stretching the adductors allows you to sit on the horse with better alignment. The better your alignment, the easier it is to turn on your deep stabilisers of your core and your pelvis.

The calf muscles

The calf muscles attach just above the knee and run down to the Achilles tendon at the back of the ankle. Generally, if your hamstrings are tight, your calves will be too. Once again, a sedentary job is the villain in the piece, but not stretching after exercise and regularly wearing high heels doesn't help matters either.

trouble downstairs

As your own awareness of how you carry your body increases, you will be more likely to identify your own incorrect lower body position. You may well see yourself now in one of these common compensatory patterns.

Thigh grip

Thigh grip is one of the most common compensations for a lack of stability in the core. Here, the adductors are the primary muscles that are firing, which causes gripping in the upper leg close to the groin area. This action also turns on the hip flexors. It is often seen in riders who lean forward, slump or who tend to sit with a swayback on the horse. Because the spine is not aligned, the adductors turn on to balance the pelvis in the saddle. This results in a cascade of reactions down the leg that compromise the position of the knee and ankle. It also precipitates a cascade further up the body that compromises upper body alignment and effectiveness.

Ideal line

Knee grip

Here the gripping is happening slightly lower down, around the knee joint. Using the knee as an anchor point is another compensation that indicates lack of core stability. Riders who are unstable use knee gripping as they work to find a stabilising point for their imbalances. It can also present a problem for those whose deep hip controllers of the leg are insufficiently strong. Riders try to influence the horse to move sideways by pressing in with the knee, rather than with the whole leg in a soft position, which must originate from the hip.

Hamstrings turned on

Switching on the hamstring muscles is something that almost all riders resort to when they try to use strong, familiar muscles to execute a leg aid. The result is that the knee opens and bends and the heel comes back. Not only are the incorrect muscles being recruited, but the effectiveness of the aids and the rider's position are compromised. This is a highly common bad habit that can occur any time an unstable rider wants to put a leg aid on.

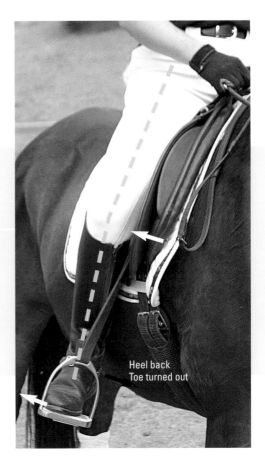

Heel back
Toe turned out

more trouble downstairs

Backward leaner with legs too far forward

Backward leaning and slumping are indirectly related. Usually, a backward leaner is a slumper who is trying to sit more upright, thereby engaging another compensation system. In this case, the pelvis is tipped forward and the bottom bones are out the front door. As this destabilises the whole pelvic area, the rider's legs come forward to counterbalance the pelvic position. It is difficult to sit with both the upper and lower body out of alignment in this way, so the legs have to grip to hold the position.

Swayback with toes turned out.

Here you can see how a typical swayback rider will often end up with her toes turned outwards. A person with a swayback posture often has permanently tightened hip flexors as the forward tilt of the pelvis pulls on these large muscles. In the saddle, the bottom bones are tipped out the back door and so the hamstring muscles are recruited to compensate. These active muscles then pull the lower leg upward and the toes point outwards in the process.

Ideal line

Legs grip to hold

Ideal line

Toe turned out

what's the ideal?

In the correct position the leg is long and relaxed, there is gentle contact with the saddle and there is no gripping or tension in any of the muscle groups of the lower body. From the side, the hip and heel are in a perfect line. Interestingly, efficient riders do require a lot of muscular strength in their legs at times. However, the difference is that when they apply this strength it originates at the hip and they use the whole leg as a unit. Good core stability and strength and flexibility in the correct leg muscles are essential to achieving that type of leg control. And for that you must do your exercises.

Ideal line

Larissa says

The most common incorrect leg position that I see in my students is heels up and too far back with the toes pointing outward. This makes them lose not only their stirrups but also the connection from a stable centre up and down the body. This is one of the most difficult incorrect positions of the lower body to fix, because no matter how often I ask my students to point the toes forward and allow their heels to come down, they can't maintain the correct position. It's only been since I have encountered the principles of stretching and strengthening the leg off the horse have I come to realise that this problem can rarely be solved in the saddle. The body's ingrained compensation patterns of turning on the hamstring muscles and gripping are just too strong. So, I would encourage anyone wanting a longer leg position to commit to working on their core stability and to stretch and strengthen their legs.

stretching a point

A useful lesson that I learnt from working with Anna-Louise on my lower body is that the body needs a combination of flexibility, strength and control for balanced alignment. Your spine and pelvis are three-dimensional structures. Stretching stiff bits is like taking a twisted Rubik's cube and then subtly adjusting one section one way and the next layer another way until it's perfectly square.

Better flexibility in your hot spots will help you to maintain balanced alignment. This in turn makes it much easier to stabilise your core and develop soft control. The goal for stretching your lower body is for your deep corset to be supportive enough to allow your legs to move independently around a stable centre while you're in the saddle. For this to become a permanent feature of your riding, you have to think of the work of increasing flexibility as being linked inextricably to the work of stabilising your core. Anna-Louise points out that stretching and stabilising are like a clutch and an accelerator: as you ease one off, you may need to increase the other. Finding what works for you takes time but the effort is well worth it in terms of achieving grounded riding for good.

There is another important reason to stretch often: it feels good!

We all need to stretch to maintain a comfortable body, but few of us do so on a regular basis. Even people who train frequently tend not to stretch enough to avoid injury and keep their bodies working freely. Stretching isn't just about lengthening muscles and tendons, it's also about taking joints through their full range of motion, which is important for keeping connective tissue nourished and healthy. It also works wonders for reducing the stiffness and strain most of us carry around in our bodies due to hours spent slumping in front of the computer or hunched over a steering-wheel.

What if I'm really stiff?
Stretching can seem a bit daunting if you're not used to it. Don't assume you're just naturally as stiff as a board and that your body is beyond redemption. Be gentle but persistent and believe that you will improve. Eventually you'll find yourself looking forward to stretching because of the way it makes your body feel so much lighter and freer.

What if I'm already flexible?
If you're one of these naturally flexible individuals who could do the splits as a child, you may enjoy stretching, find it comes easily to you and spend more time doing that than anything else. In fact, you need to focus more on your stability exercises, as people who are generally looser have to rely heavily on their deep corset to keep them stable due to their loose ligaments.

A few guidelines for stretching

- As a general rule, muscles respond better to stretching when they are warm. Doing some gentle activity or having a warm shower before you start will improve the effectiveness of the stretches.

- You may find it helpful to perform your stretches in front of a mirror to check your form.

- Stretch to a point at which you feel tension and a slight pulling sensation in the targeted muscle but no pain. Never bounce or force a stretched position. Remember that none of the stretching exercises in this book should be painful. If you're uncertain if any of them are suitable for you, consult your GP or physiotherapist.

- Gently hold the position for 30 to 60 seconds—or longer if you have the time or can bear it. You have to hold long enough for the 'stress-relaxation' response to occur and the force on the muscle to decrease. Release and then repeat. You will often find that you can go a bit deeper into the stretch the second time.

- Breathe deeply to engage your deep corset fully. If you're finding the stretch fairly intense, pay attention to your breath and make sure it's not getting stuck in your upper chest giving rise to unwanted tension in your neck and shoulders. Allow yourself to release muscle tension on each exhalation. Let go. Breathe.

- Make sure you do it regularly. The benefits accrue the more often you stretch, so you may have to designate specific times to devote to your exercises. After a riding session is a clear opportunity to loosen tight muscles that may have been used to compensate for imbalances. It's also a good idea to stretch after long hours of sitting. A tried-and-true strategy for finding time to stretch is to do so while you're watching one of your favourite TV programs.

- Remember that if your muscles are tight because of postural imbalances that you have had for many years, it will take commitment and time for them to become looser. Keep at it.

- While it is ideal to stretch just before you ride, this isn't always practical. So, it's important to do these stretches a few times a week to ensure you are freeing up your tight muscles to help you maintain your new, balanced alignment. You'll find your riding begins to improve as you can then transfer this new alignment to the saddle.

sitting hip and buttock stretch

This is a simple but powerful stretch that can be done at any time of the day when you are sitting around.

Equipment

- a chair
- posture dots

What to do

- Attach your posture dots and sit on balanced bottom bones on the edge of a chair.
- Cross your right ankle over your left knee. Try to keep your hips as level as possible.
- Raise your arms up over your head and stretch upwards.
- Now, without bending through your back or slumping, lean forwards and upwards as far as possible. When you feel a strong stretch feeling in your right hip and buttock, stop.
- Breathe in slowly. As you breathe out, slowly lower your arms, keeping your centre dot lifted.

- Gently put your right elbow into the inside of the right knee and press down a little to increase the stretch. If it feels more comfortable, just place your right hand on your knee.
- Sit in this position for 30 to 60 seconds while breathing slowly before repeating on the other side.

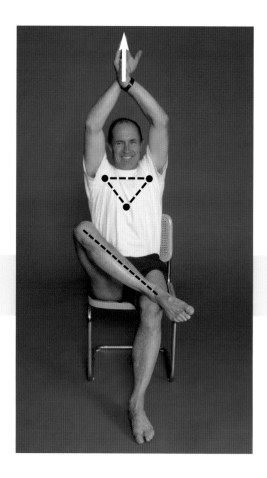

Focus

You may find that one side feels more flexible than the other. If this is the case, repeat the stretch twice on the stiffer side. This stretch targets a small muscle deep in the hips called the piriformis. It is a particularly important one for riders because when it functions well it allows greater freedom in the hip when you are on the horse. This in turn takes the load off your lower back and makes it easier to maintain your core stability.

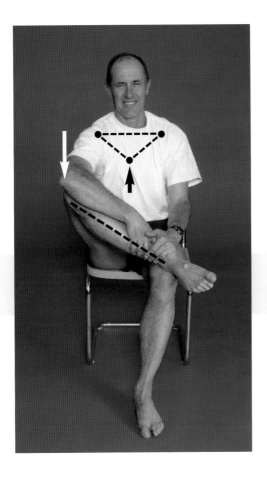

We all have to stretch

Tightness in the body happens to everyone. Professional riders who spend hours each day in the saddle develop tightness that needs to be stretched. Larissa finds that one hip gets tighter than the other, that her adductors feel tight sometimes and that stiffness sometimes sets in around old injury sights.

She finds that this hip and buttock stretch provides instant relief whenever she needs it.

the Lancelot stretch

If you're a rider who can't seem to get your leg long, chances are your psoas muscles are tight, which keeps the upper leg in a shortened position. This is a great stretch to lengthen out these strong muscles. Anna Louise calls it the Lancelot stretch because you begin as if you are about to be knighted.

Equipment
- posture dots
- a mirror

What to do
- Attach your posture dots and kneel in front of a mirror with your left leg in front.
- Check your alignment and set yourself up on train tracks.
- Raise your arms up over your head and stretch upwards as in the sitting hip and buttock stretch.
- Now, tilt your pelvis under by imagining that your pubic bone is moving towards your nose.
- Squeeze your right buttock as hard as you can while you stretch your torso upwards. You should feel a stretch down the front of the right hip and leg. Hold for 30 seconds at least while breathing slowly.
- Take a deep breath in. As you exhale, lower your arms to rest on your thigh.
- Hold the stretch for another 30 seconds before repeating on the other side.

Incorrect

Focus

Make sure that both your front and back knees are at perfect 90° angles. Keep your centre dot lifted and your shoulders and neck relaxed. Keep the working buttock firm. If your supporting knee hurts, place a towel under it. Once again, you may find that one side feels more flexible than the other. If so, repeat the stretch twice on the stiffer side. Can you make a link between stiffness on one side and anything that is happening in your riding?

Incorrect

psoas stretch

This is another deep stretch that brings relief to your tight, overloaded psoas. You can do this one in addition to or instead of the Lancelot to loosen up this most important muscle group.

Equipment
- posture dots
- a mirror

What to do
- Attach your posture dots and start as for the Lancelot with the left knee directly over your heel. Gently extend the right heel back until the knee comes off the ground no more than 5 cm.
- Place your hands on either side of the left foot and keep your body weight over the left leg.
- Look up and allow your groin area to sink down towards the floor, feeling the stretch at the front of the hip. Extend your heel back while keeping your centre dot lifted.
- Hold this position for 30 to 60 seconds at least while breathing slowly before repeating on the other side.

Focus
Make sure your back knee is slightly bent but don't let it touch the floor. Be careful not to overbend the front knee. Keep it over the heel at a 90° angle. Make sure you're not tensing your neck and shoulders.

Incorrect

Calling all swaybacks

If you have a swayback, you will have tightness in your hips. This stretch is especially valuable for you. Make time for it as often as you can. If you can improve the flexibility in your psoas you will find it easier to stabilise your alignment.

Ideal Line

hamstring stretch

This is not a traditional hamstring stretch but it is most effective. One of the biggest problems with stretching is that our bodies are very clever at taking the path of least resistance. As a result you will often end up stretching the wrong muscles or placing stress on your body without realising it. Done correctly, this stretch ensures you really get to the hamstrings safely.

It is also a wonderful back reliever as it stretches the muscles deep in the buttocks and at the top of the hamstrings. And it's excellent for riders because it lengthens these muscles allowing them to be freer and less tense in the legs when riding.

Equipment
- a chair
- posture dots

What to do
- Attach your posture dots and start by placing your left foot up on a chair.
- Reach under your buttocks and grab your bottom bones.
- Keep your centre dot lifted as you bend forward, pulling your bottom bones up and keeping your back straight.

- When you feel a strong stretch feeling in the back of your leg, stop. Now, reach forward and put your hands on the back of the chair.
- Make sure your left nipple is in line with your left knee.
- Breathe in. As you breathe out, rotate the leg outwards about 20°.
- Sink deeper into your support leg and lean back slightly to increase the stretch.
- Hold this position for 30 to 60 seconds at least while breathing slowly before repeating on the other side.

Focus
Make sure that when you lean foward you actually pull your bottom bones with you, not just your flesh. Keep the leg in front at an angle greater than 90°. As before, stretch your stiffer side twice more than your more flexible side.

anti-gravity hamstring stretch

Got very tight hamstrings and a spare 10 minutes? Then this is the stretch for you. Sometimes it is effective to let gravity do the work to stretch out muscles that have been tight for a very long time.

Equipment
• a solid wall against which to put your legs

What to do
• Lie down and put your feet up against the wall.

• Slide your bottom as close to the wall as possible. If you are very stiff, you may need to put a rolled-up towel under your hips to get close enough.

• Make sure to line your legs up like two train tracks and that they are straight from the heels through the knees down to the hips. Don't let your feet turn out.

• Now just lie quietly and imagine your hamstrings stretching.

• Every once and a while gently pull your toes down towards your shins, increasing the stretch.

• When you are ready to get up, bend your knees and roll on to your side.

Focus
While your hamstring muscles are stretching, take some time to do focused breathing, activating your deep corset with each out breath. Then, do some visual imagery of riding with a stable core. Visualise your arms and legs working softly and independently around your stable centre. Imagine that your legs are long and powerful and that you can influence your horse with only the smallest of aids. Enjoy this focus time—you and your horse are sure to benefit.

lying adductor stretch

The strong muscles of the inner thighs often become tight when we ride. All riders know that uncomfortable feeling—especially if you have had some time off. After the first few rides back, these muscles can feel really stiff and even ache. Here is a great way to give them a good stretch.

What to do

- Start lying down on your back.
- Bend your knees up with your feet resting on the floor.
- Try to keep the soles of your feet together as you let your legs flop out to the sides.
- Watch that your back does not arch too far. Keep it in the balanced position.
- Hold this position as you relax and imagine that your adductors are lengthening.

Focus

You can easily focus on activating your deep corset while you are doing this adductor stretch. Simply bring your attention to your breathing, and on each slow exhalation, imagine that you are drawing the pelvic floor muscles up into the body. This combines two great exercises in one!

on-all-fours adductor stretch

This adductor stretch is performed on all fours. It provides an intense stretch, so move into the position gently.

What to do

- Kneel on all fours.

- Drop your upper body down so you are resting on your elbows. Your bottom will now be sticking up in the air slightly.

- Try to keep the soles of your feet together as you slowly spread your knees outwards so that the weight of your body helps you stretch out the adductors.

- Keep sliding the knees out until you feel a good stretch in this area.

- Now just relax in this position, take some deep breaths and imagine the muscles lengthening.

Focus

This is another position that you can use to focus on activating your pelvic floor. Allow your body to relax. Feel the adductors stretching as you pay attention to your breath. Breathe in to a slow count of 4 and as you breathe out to a slow count of 4, imagine drawing up the pea in the straw or lifting the jewels off the saddle.

strength and control

Increasing your flexibility in your lower body is only one part of the process of acquiring the ability to use your whole leg as a unit while on the horse. The other parts involve building strength and learning how to control the muscles you require to ride better. This way your brain fully comprehends what you are setting out to achieve, making it much more likely that you will absorb and apply new skills.

What's in a buttock?

The buttocks play a vital role not only in controlling our hips, but in coordinating our trunk and leg movement.

Most of us think of our buttocks as being two big muscles that sit (often not very firmly!) at the top of our legs. In fact, as we have seen, the buttocks are made up of a series of muscles which are arranged in layers.

Each muscle layer plays a specific role in controlling hip movement and consequently influences the alignment and stability of the trunk. If the muscles of the buttocks are weak, the hip area can become unstable. So, strengthening the buttocks contributes to maintaining good core stability.

Many of us have never felt the specific action of controlling our deeper buttock muscles to influence our leg movements. To do this, we have to re-establish motor pathways to these deeper muscles in order to use them more effectively in the saddle.

Say hello to your gluteus maximus

The gluteus maximus is the most superficial muscle of the buttock complex. It is a global muscle like many of the other large, superficial muscles in the body. It extends down from your sacrum (the boniest part of your low back) to the point at which your buttock joins your leg. Its role is to extend the hip and push you forward when you walk. When it works well it is like a retro-rocket for your trunk.

Because many of us spend more time sitting on our gluteus maximus than using it, it often becomes weak and loses tone. You will know if this has happened to you by just feeling it. If poking your bottom feels more like pushing into a sponge than a firm melon, then it is likely that you are not activating this muscle as well as you could.

There are also a small percentage of people who naturally have a poorly developed gluteus maximus. This is an inherited condition that results in a very flat bottom. Many women with this small gluteus maximus will complain they can never find pants to fit them as there is always too much fabric in the bottom. Men with this flat bottom tend to have trouble holding their pants up at the back. Anecdotally, this inherited shape seems to contribute to difficulty activating the muscle.

The effects of a weak gluteus maximus

There are several ways to tell if a person is insufficiently activating their gluteus maximus. Walking tends to be more slumped and the person looks as if they are dragging themselves along rather than striding purposely forward. This is because the hip is not being efficiently extended by the gluteus maximus.

On the horse the gluteus maximus is vital for controlling both your up/down movement and your forward/back movement. One of the best examples of this is in the canter. Think of the often-used analogy, 'polish the saddle with your bottom'. In this action, your gluteus maximus is the muscle responsible for the gentle rocking motion of the hips. When the gluteus maximus is weak the rider will subconsciously compensate by bringing in the next available global muscle, which is likely to be the hamstrings. If you grip with your hamstrings in the canter, your bottom will come up out of the saddle, your feet will roll outwards and your heels will come up. You won't be able to make a solid connection between your seat and the horse.

Another example of the effects of a weak gluteus maximus is in the rising trot. Tilting forward, being too rigid, losing your stirrups, gripping with your knees or doing a 'double bounce' when you hit the saddle are all the result of the leg muscles trying to organise the movement instead of the gluteus maximus. When it is working as it should, it slightly contracts with each rise, giving you a forward momentum and greater effectiveness as you rise out of the saddle in balance with your horse.

A strong gluteus maximus gives you the power you need to drive your horse forward, to maintain a good connection in the saddle, to keep your horse active in the collected work and to be balanced and grounded when you ride.

bottom clenching

This exercise serves two purposes. It teaches you to feel how your gluteus maximus works, waking up your awareness of this important muscle, and it strengthens it at the same time. Don't just do 'Bottom clenching' as a specific exercise. It's something you can do any time of day—you just might want to omit the clenching device when in public.

Equipment
- bottom clencher or credit card
- posture dots
- a mirror

What to do
- Attach your posture dots.
- Stand facing your mirror with feet shoulder width apart and parallel.
- Unlock your knees and lift your dots.
- Find the balanced position of your spine.
- Hold your credit card, or bottom clencher, in your right hand with your index finger on one of the short sides.

- Relax your buttocks then gently place the card between your cheeks.
- Keep your knees soft and unlocked and hold the card there for at least 60 seconds.

Focus
Relax the rest of your body and lift your dots as you clench your gluteus maximus to keep the card in place. Breathe in and out slowly as you squeeze it. Be very careful not to let your feet rotate outwards. This is cheating.

bottom walking

Strong buttock muscles mean stronger walking with a longer stride and less movement through the trunk. Turning one buttock off while turning the other on is the key to effective muscle control when walking. This exercise shows you how to recruit your glutes while walking. Once you become proficient at it, you can practise it all day.

Equipment
- posture dots

What to do
- Attach your posture dots.
- Stand as if you're about to take a step, with your right leg forward with the heel about to hit the ground and your left leg back.
- Lift your dots. Keep your left leg relaxed.
- Put your hand on your left buttock.
- Transfer your weight forward on to the right leg by contracting the left buttock.
- Imagine your left buttock is pushing your weight forward on to the right foot. Keep the knees soft.
- Transfer the weight back on to the left leg and let the left buttock relax.
- Repeat 15 to 20 times on this leg, turning the buttock on to go forward and off to transfer back, before changing to the other leg.

Focus
Be careful not to stiffen your knees. Make sure your head is steady and that you're not swaying from side to side. Always lead strongly with your heel to trigger the buttock muscles. When you feel familiar with this action of propelling yourself forward with the buttock of your back leg, work on building up speed so that you can apply it whenever you walk. All lateral riding movements require the ability to turn on one side of the body while leaving the other relaxed, and this is a good introduction to this skill while off the horse.

digging deeper

The gluteus medius and minimus make up the deeper layers of the gluteal complex. They are postural muscles and as such they are recruited to provide control. If you put your finger into the side of your buttock and press firmly you will feel a tender spot. This is approximately the position of these muscles. Because of their location and function they control both the 'side to side' movement of your pelvis and the rotation of your leg from the hip. Their role is to control the alignment of the leg relative to the pelvis. Because of this, we'll call them the deep hip controllers. While walking they activate to keep your pelvis level and stable as you step onto your leg.

Weakness in the deep hip controllers

Sloppy walking, standing slumped onto one leg all the time, sitting with your legs crossed... these are all postural habits off the horse that contribute to the weakening of these deep muscles.

This results in the muscles dropping the hip sideways, which doesn't just affect the hip. It means that as you walk, you 'unlock' the hip sideways instead of landing on a stable leg. You compensate for this further by the low back moving sideways in the opposite direction. This in turn makes it difficult to keep the low back stable. In effect, landing on an unstable hip and trying to keep your low back stable is like standing up in a little rowboat. If the base is unstable the job of maintaining stability higher up is made even harder.

Weakness and riding

While riding, the role of these muscles is to control the alignment of the leg relative to the trunk thus allowing the whole leg to be controlled from the hip. This concept is often expressed by some of the world's greatest riders by the simple statement 'put your leg on from the hip', but it's very difficult to grasp if you have never experienced the feeling of using your inner gluteal muscles in the saddle.

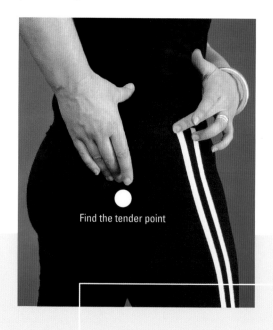

Find the tender point

Because the base is constantly moving while riding, the ability to maintain your deep stability and alignment in both your trunk and hips is crucial. To do this effectively you require these deep buttock muscles to control the position of your leg.

When they are working efficiently, you can remain grounded in the saddle and make subtle changes of pressure in your seat to use them to control the horse. You can put your leg aids on more effectively from the hip, and greatly improve your ability to change the direction of the horse while maintaining your hip and trunk alignment.

When they are weak, you tend to compensate by using other global muscles in the leg, knee and foot to control the leg alignment. This is like trying to ride from the feet up instead of the seat down.

Finding your deep hip controllers

To locate your deep hip controllers, you need to find the soft spot just on the top and to the side of your buttock. If you press gently in, it will feel a bit tender. Have a look at the photo with the dots on the backside. This is their approximate location. To feel them in the exercises, you need to dig a bit deep!

activating your deep hip controllers

Now that you've identified your deep hip controllers you have to learn how to switch them on. This exercise really wakes up the deep muscles used to initiate leg movements in the saddle.

Equipment
- posture dots
- a mirror

What to do
- Attach posture dots to your hip and knee.
- Place your hands on your buttocks with your fingertips pushing into the area of your deep hip controllers.
- Place your right foot one step in front of your left.
- Take a deep breath in and, without moving the foot, rotate the right leg inwards.
- Breathe out slowly thinking of the drawing up feeling of your pelvic floor muscles as you move your leg outwards.
- Breathe in, leg rotates inward. Breathe out, leg rotates outwards.

- Make sure you are not just moving your knee, but focus on feeling the deep glute muscles working with your fingertips. You may have to move your fingers a bit to find these muscles if you don't feel anything at first.
- Repeat 15 to 20 times on each leg.

Focus
This movement is very subtle and it can take some practice before you are sure of it. To start with you may find you're initiating it by simply moving the knee, which is what we tend to do on the horse. Because the deep buttock muscles are closely linked with your pelvic floor muscles, it really helps to coordinate the action with your breathing. This also links your core control with your hip control, a vital feature of good riding.

stronger legs

After you have gained better control of the deep internal rotators, the next step is to build strength. One very effective way of doing this is to perform the exercise for activating the leg rotators with an exercise band around your calves for resistance. Don't try this until you are sure that you have mastered control of those muscles. You may be surprised at the extra challenge provided by a strong piece of elasticised band.

Equipment
- exercise band
- posture dots
- a mirror

What to do
- Attach posture dots to your hips and knees. Tie the exercise band around your calves.
- Place your right foot in front of your left and your hands on your buttocks with your fingertips pushing into the dots. Use the mirror to make sure that your hip, knee and toe are aligned.
- Take a deep breath in while moving your leg inwards from the hip.
- Slowly breathe out while drawing up your pelvic floor muscles as the leg rotates outwards from the hip.

- The rotation movement is initiated in the deep buttock and allows the knee to move outwards. Be conscious that your leg is moving against the resistance. Use your fingers to feel your glutes firing.
- Repeat 15 to 20 times on each leg.

Focus
As a rule, you should always exhale with the exertion or more difficult part of any exercise. In this instance, it's especially important that your breathing is correct: breathe in as the leg moves inwards and breathe out as it moves outwards. This really grounds your core stability and allows the leg to work without any compensating movement. Practise in front of a mirror to ensure that your alignment remains intact. To start with, do as many as you can and stop if your muscles fatigue. Build up to 20 repetitions.

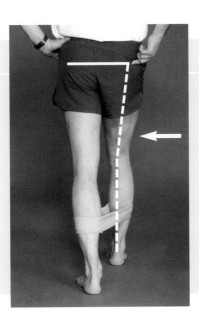 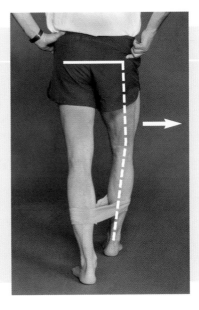

lying hip control

The next progression is to perform this exercise lying down with the exercise band tied around your foot and a table leg. This increases the challenge considerably. In the beginning, I could only do about 10 repetitions without really feeling tired. You should build up to doing 15 to 20 repetitions on each leg. This only takes a few minutes—imagine the strength that these muscles require for a one-hour training session on the horse!

Equipment
- posture dots
- a strong table
- exercise band

What to do
- Attach posture dots to your hips, knees and toe.
- Attach the exercise band around the leg of a table and your left foot.
- Lie back with your left leg partially extended (in riding position) and your right leg bent with the foot on the floor.
- Take a deep breath in. As you breathe out move your leg inwards while thinking of drawing the pelvic floor muscles into the body. Inhale and move it outwards.
- Keep your neck and shoulders relaxed.
- Repeat 5 to 10 times before changing around to the other leg. Build to 15 to 20 repetitions as you become stronger. It's better to do fewer repetitions well than more repetitions badly.

Focus
Whenever the body finds something difficult to control it often uses completely unrelated muscles to help out. When I started to do this exercise, my initial reaction was to lift my opposite shoulder to compensate for the work in my hip. My body awareness told me that this was most likely also happening on the horse! Make sure that you concentrate during this exercise, work in a very small range of motion and link the action with your breathing. This will guarantee better core stability and allow the leg movement to happen without any compensatory reaction in the upper body.

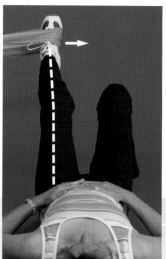

seated hip control

After practice in the lying position, this exercise can be done in a seated position using a bar stool or saddle type seat.

Eqipment

- bar stool or saddle chair
- table
- exercise band

What to do

- Attach the exercise band around the leg of a table and your right foot.
- Sit on the stool and lift your dots.
- Take a deep breath in. As you exhale, move your leg inwards. Focus on drawing up the pelvic floor muscles into the body. Inhale and allow the leg to move outwards.
- Repeat 5 to 10 times before changing around to the other leg. Build up to 15 to 20 good repetitions on each side.

Focus

Once you sit upright like this, you may notice that your body wants to compensate in new ways. I wanted to initiate the action by turning my foot out and using my hamstring muscles. I am sure this was happening in the saddle. If you stay aware of your breathing and activate your core, you will be able to do the exercise with integrity and good alignment, which will then transfer to better use of your whole leg when riding.

Incorrect

part three
Soft riding

Lisa's story

My initial sessions with Anna Louise had focused very much on activating my core muscles and doing exercises to make my legs work more independently. Now it was time to work on the upper body.

One of the key limitations to effective movement that Anna Louise notices in many people, from riders to footballers to sedentary workers, is lack of control at the base leading to the recruitment of muscles higher up the chain to compensate. For riders this means that if we lack stability in the saddle, we will try to gain control by making the upper body 'stiffer' or more stable.

I was conscious that this applied to me. When in the saddle I felt frustrated by my inability to apply subtle rein aids. I'd ask myself why did it feel like I had to balance myself with a strong rein contact? Why did the reins keep getting 'pulled' out of my hands? Why was it that every time I did a half-halt, my upper body moved forward as I gave? Why was it that I couldn't seem to get my elbows back by my sides and that sometimes my arms were too straight? Why did Larissa keep commenting that my hands were moving up and down and my elbows seemed too rigid? Oh, if only having the head knowledge would make my body cooperate!

In fact, Anna Louise identified that the same thing was happening with my upper body as with my lower. I lacked the ability to move my arms independently and softly because I didn't have the core stability to stay balanced in the saddle without a strong rein contact. Also, I was unable use my arms without compensatory movement in the rest of my body. Even with my developing sense of core stability, I still had some ingrained movement patterns that needed to be replaced with more effective ones that used my deep corset as a basis of dynamic stability.

Ask yourself this

- How much do you concentrate on the horse's head position compared with what's happening at the tail end?

- If you were to express as a percentage the amount of emphasis you place on your upper body and arms versus your lower body, seat and legs when you ride, what would it be?

For many riders, the percentage for upper body emphasis (for both themselves and the horse) would be higher than for the lower body. Improving your core stability will allow you to sit more balanced and effectively in the saddle so that you can reverse this. You will be able to place more emphasis on what's happening in your seat and legs and on what's happening in the engine-room of your horse.

arms behaving badly

What are some of the most common problems with the head, shoulders, arms and hands when we ride? Have a look at the photos and see if you recognise any of these habits.

Arms too straight

This compensation can be seen in both slumpers and swaybacks when the rider uses rein contact to find a balance point for the unstable body. If these riders lack strength in the upper back and are unstable in their centre, the weight of the horse's head and neck will inevitably 'pull' their arms into a straighter position. They may find that their reins get longer and longer as they ride, their arms grow very tired and that they can't sufficiently 'give' the rein, making an effective half-halt very difficult.

Elbows out

This position is very common with riders who slump. You may not be aware that you are a slumper, but if your elbows stick out when you ride, it's a dead giveaway. When you slump, the shoulders are rounded and forward and, as a consequence, the elbows come out. A response to this is the hand flattening, with the thumbs pointing inward, rather than being on top. Correcting this is not just a matter of holding the elbows in. The problem lies in the slumped position of the trunk, which causes certain muscles to be weak and tightened, thus forcing the elbows to compensate.

Driving the car

Does your riding instructor ever tell you that one hand sits higher than the other most of the time? Do you notice that your hands tend to look like you are 'driving a car' rather than staying in alignment with the horse's body as you go around a corner or ride a circle? If so, it's likely that you are a sideways curver and that one shoulder tends to sit higher than the other. This is reflected in the hand position, as the hand of the higher shoulder will also sit higher.

Inside hand coming up and over the wither

This incorrect alignment in the upper body usually reflects a lack of core stability and effective control and strength in the lower body. When the horse is not moving off the inside leg (because the aid is not effective) the rider will try to compensate by lifting the hand up and over the wither. This is especially noticeable when attempting shoulder-in and half-pass. While this riding habit is most prevalent in sideways curvers, it appears with all incorrect postural types who lack core stability and leg strength and control.

head case

Slumpers have the greatest tendency to look down, but it can also become a habit of any rider who becomes fixated on the horse's head and neck position. Looking down sends a chain of flexion responses through the body. As the chin comes towards the chest, the shoulders round and come forward and the body collapses in the middle which causes the lower legs to slide back to compensate. It's amazing how many riders never realise that with their head up they still have enormous range of vision—just by moving their eyes!

what's the ideal?

We all know what the ideal upper body position is when we see it. There is a straight line between the elbow, hand and bit, the elbow is softly bent and close to the rider's side and the alignment of the upper body stays even and correct, regardless of the position the rider is putting the horse into. But how do we achieve this ideal?

It starts with the foundation of good core stability and then the addition of effective lower body strength and control, as we have established. Then, there's a three-step process re-lated specifically to your upper body that is the same as we've seen with your lower body:

1 stretching
2 strengthening
3 gaining control.

And that's what this section is about.

Many of the problems we have with the upper body are associated with slumping. All postural types tend to slump at times, partly because our sedentary lives provides us with so many opportunities to do so. Once we let our shoulders and head come forward, gravity is only too ready to push us downwards further. The forward, rounded shoulder position caused by slumping leads to stiffness and weakness in the thoracic spine, which is the area in your mid to upper back. Loosening up the mid-back allows the load to be distributed more evenly along your whole spine. This eases discomfort and also improves your habitual incorrect riding positions. So, the next thing to do is add some upper body stretches to your program.

seated chair twist & saddle twist

This simple exercise really targets the tight muscles between your shoulder blades and eases tension in the shoulders and neck. It's a good idea to do this regularly if you're engaged in prolonged bouts of sitting to prevent your spine from stiffening up. It can be performed very easily in the saddle and is a useful complement to a riding session. If you're a slumper, or if you just have stiffness in your mid-back, try doing this stretch several times to each side before you begin your ride.

Equipment
- a chair
- posture dots
- a mirror

What to do
- Attach your posture dots.
- Position the chair sideways on to the mirror. Sit forward on the edge of the chair with balanced bottom bones.

- Place your left hand across your right knee with your palm away from you. Place your right hand into the inside of the back of the chair and push through the palm.
- Bend your right elbow until your right shoulder relaxes and the right posture dot becomes level with the left one.
- Take a deep breath in. As you breathe out, gently turn your body to the right. Hold for 10 seconds.
- Breathe in again and push a little further as you breathe out. Hold for 30 seconds then slowly return to centre.
- Repeat on the other side.

Focus

Soften the back shoulder rather than lifting it and keep your neck relaxed and long. Make sure your dots stay even and your deep corset is activated. If you slump in the twist position you'll notice that your dots no longer make a nice level triangle. Keep your chin tucked slightly in and in line with your sternum as you twist. If your head turns more than your chest you can strain your neck muscles. Always look for ways to release tension when you stretch, not increase it.

When Larissa sees a student dropping the outside shoulder going into shoulder-in, she has them stop riding shoulder-in and change to a leg yielding on the wall with outside flexion, moving the horse's quarters to the inside. In essence, by changing the position to ride the leg yield, she gets the rider to do a modified saddle twist while riding.

If you feel uncomfortable between the shoulder blades in this stretch, turn your chair sideways and position your hands like this.

table stretch

This stretch not only lengthens and relaxes the thoracic spine but also the lower back. It's a real tonic for your spine. You can do it holding on to a fence, which makes it another useful exercise to perform just before or after a riding session. This is now Larissa's favourite stretch.

Equipment
- balcony rail or fence rail (or anything else sturdy enough to support your weight), about 1 m high

What to do
- Place your hands on your table-stretch anchor.
- Slowly walk back until you feel your armpits stretch and the sides of your waist extend.
- Keep your feet together and your knees soft. Your feet should be slightly under your body.

- Extend your bottom as far away from your hands as you can without letting your back arch. If your thoracic spine is very stiff, it will be difficult for you at first to achieve a flat back in this position.
- Hold for 30 to 60 seconds while breathing deeply.

Incorrect

Ideal line

Focus

Keep your weight in the heels and the legs re-laxed. If you have a naturally swayback you can overarch in this position, which puts too much stress on your shoulders. On the other hand, if your legs are too straight and your back is too rounded, you will not feel the lovely stretch underneath your armpits. You have to unlock your knees, sink into the heels and lengthen your back for the stretch to work.

Working **miracles**

To test the effectiveness of this stretch, first bend over and see how far down towards your toes you can reach. Make a mental note. Perform the table stretch and then try again. You'll be amazed at the difference.

upper body strength

Have a look at the photo showing slumping posture from behind. Notice how the back widens, the shoulders are forward, the head is forward and the waist has expanded? Not a good look! Have a look now at the balanced bottom bones posture from behind. See how the shoulders come up and back, making them more level? Notice how the head is poised on top of the neck where it belongs? Note the thinning of the waist and how much taller and open the body becomes. So which muscles must we strengthen to maintain this?

It's the muscles of the upper back, in particular your trapezius (the diamond-shaped muscle that runs from the back of your neck down into your upper back) and your rhomboids (between your shoulder blades). To maintain a balanced spine, not only does your deep corset have to be effective but these upper body muscles also have to perform a vital balancing act.

When we slump the rhomboids become weak, which causes them to wing out to the sides creating rounded shoulders. To compensate for this, the upper part of the trapezius muscle works extra hard and tightens up—think of that rock hard muscle just behind your shoulder running toward your neck. While the top of the trapezius is slaving away, the lower part, near your shoulder blades, slackens and becomes increasingly weak. To reverse the damage of this chain reaction, we have to im-prove the efficiency of those muscles that are weak.

We also need to focus our attention on our upper arms, so that we combine improved strength in both the upper back and the arms to create a more balanced body, able to cope with the dynamic demands of riding. The biceps muscles (as in Popeye) are especially important here as they are prime movers when we bend our elbows. For most people it's that bending action that is the hard part of training the biceps. But for riders, the critical part of the movement is control during the return movement. This is related to the fact that we require the greatest core stability when our limbs are lengthening or moving away from the body. If we don't have good strength to make the bend, and then good control when we let the bend go, we will never have truly effective rein aids.

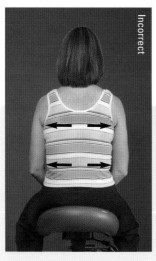
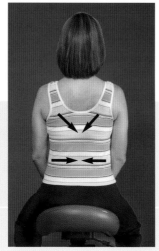

Incorrect

bent-over row

This strengthening exercise works the muscles in the arms and upper back that are directly responsible for the 'taking' action of the rein, especially when the elbow moves behind the body. It also improves strength in the upper back for less slumping and better upper body alignment. The return part of the movement provides an opportunity to practise good core control as the arm moves away from the body.

Equipment
- exercise band (if you don't have one, this exercise can also be done with a dumbbell or even holding a big bag of rice)
- a mirror

What to do
- Turn side-on to the mirror keeping the arm you are working towards it.
- Place your left foot about 30 cm in front of the right and bend your knees slightly.
- Divide the exercise band evenly and place your left foot into the centre.
- Wrap each side of the band around your hands, and place your left hand on your slightly bent left thigh.
- Breathe in. As you breathe out, straighten your right arm towards the floor as you can see in the first photograph.

- Breathe in and bend the elbow, drawing the hand up towards your waist. Keep your elbow close to your side.
- Keep your shoulders level and only turn your head to check your alignment in the mirror.
- Breathe out, drawing up your pelvic floor as you lower the hand back down.
- Repeat 12 to 15 times on each side.

Focus
Adjust the tension on the exercise band by wrapping or unwrapping extra band around your hand. You want to feel muscular fatigue in your upper arm and between your shoulder blades by the time you have done 12 to 15 repetitions. This indicates your muscles are being overloaded, which will cause them to increase their endurance. There is a direct relationship between this movement of the arm and taking and giving the rein while keeping the rest of your body stable.

soft arms

Anna-Louise originally developed this exercise to help computer-users relax their necks and keep their shoulders in a balanced position as they use the mouse. She has also used it with the NSW Waratahs to teach them how to use their arms more independently on the rugby field. For riders this exercise teaches us to soften our arms and to gain independent arm action in the saddle. The sense of upper body control you can develop from it adds another layer of skill to your improved upper body posture and position in the saddle.

Equipment
- fitball or chair
- posture dots
- a mirror

What to do
- Sit on the edge of your fitball or chair, balance your bottom bones and place your feet about riding distance apart. Check that your feet are parallel, as if on train tracks.

- Lift your dots.

- Find the balanced shoulder position for your right arm (see box below).

- Keep your right shoulder in this position with your right elbow bent and just slightly away from your side.

- Breathe in. As you slowly breathe out, imagine drawing the pea up the straw or the jewels off the saddle. At the same time, move your arm in a soft, gentle swaying motion, making a figure 8 shape in the air.

- The elbow can move slightly, but not too far away from the body.

- Develop a breathing rhythm and move your arm softly in time with the breath.

- Repeat 15 to 20 times on each side, but stop before then if you feel your body beginning to compensate.

Focus
The goal is to move the arm with an open, level shoulder position and without compensatory movement in the upper body, legs or torso. I find I can tell much more accurately if I am compensating somewhere when I do this exercise sitting on a fitball, although it is still effective on a chair, when standing or even sitting in the saddle. The mirror will help you when you first get started. Be careful not to hold your breath and use your mind to focus on moving the arm around a stable core.

I was amazed at how difficult it was to move my arm softly. At first I stiffened through the whole upper body and held my breath. I had to constantly remind myself to soften through the shoulders and back and allow my body to feel stable through the core. Interestingly,

Find your **balanced shoulder** position

Because most of us have poor posture, our shoulders tend to sit forward and up. To find your balanced shoulder position, lightly place your left hand on the front of your right shoulder. Looking down at the shoulder, gently move it back 3 cm from your fingers (don't move your hand) and lift your centre dot. Take one breath in and out and relax your neck. This is the balanced position of your shoulder.

it was easier for me to make a smooth, rhythmical pattern with my right arm than my left. This matched one of my riding issues: I found riding on the right rein more comfortable than the left.

Have a look at the incorrect variations of this exercise. In the first one, Anna-Louise is moving through her whole body and her core is unstable and wobbly. In the second one, she is lifting her shoulder to perform the movement, rather than keeping her shoulder in its balanced position.

the horse simulator

Once you've mastered 'Soft arms', it's time to practise control with a bit of resistance. By adding the feel of the reins with the exercise band, you'll build your awareness of keeping your body steady while applying rein aids. Anna-Louise developed this exercise for me because my opposite shoulder would come forward to compensate when I asked my horse for more bend. This same pattern happens in an incorrectly ridden shoulder-in. If you try to create the shoulder-in by pulling on the inside rein, your outside shoulder will often come forward and down and, to compensate, the inside leg will move too far back. When your shoulders stay level and balanced, the inside leg is able to stay long and effective. This is the perfect exercise to practise this.

Equipment

- a fitball or chair
- posture dots
- a mirror
- exercise band

What to do

- Wrap the exercise band around the leg of a table, slightly lower than waist height. Hold both ends like reins.
- Adjust the tension so that it feels as close to a riding contact as possible.
- Sit on balanced bottom bones on the fitball or the edge of the chair with your feet about riding distance apart. Check that your feet are on their train tracks.
- Lift your dots.
- Before you start the movement, take a few deep breaths, imagining the drawing up feeling of your pelvic floor with each out breath.
- Breathe in and draw one elbow back, keeping the shoulders level and the core stable. Breathe out, controlling the body as the arm lengthens slightly, and breathe in as the arm bends again.
- Repeat 15 to 20 times on each side.

Focus

Keep your neck relaxed and your shoulders soft and level. Think of using the same muscles that you used in the 'Bent-over row' to initiate the action of drawing your elbow back. Use your stable core to keep your spine balanced and your upper body still while you move the arm.

Incorrect

Look for compensations in the body. In the first photo, notice how my pelvis is rotating and my upper body twists as I bring my arm back. In the second one, notice how my opposite shoulder comes forward in response to the movement. This was something that I knew was happening to me in the saddle, although it was a very subtle action. In the third one, my sideways curve is kicking in and I am 'driving the car' instead of keeping the shoulders and upper body level. If you find your body compensating in any way, stop and have a rest or switch to the other side. It's better to do fewer repetitions perfectly than many badly.

Remember, the compensations in these shots are exaggerated. When we ride, the incorrect actions are more subtle, but not difficult to feel if we know what to look for. Lots of practice off the horse will set up new motor patterns in your body when you get back in the saddle. This mental and physical rehearsal is a critical part of training your brain to redirect the messages it sends to your muscles.

Once you've got the hang of the movement, you can play around with the degree of rein contact. Practise the three levels of contact that Larissa describes below. Try just using your hands to give a rein aid, then using a small wrist action, then doing a full arm movement—the whole time focusing on your stable core.

Larissa says

I find that many of my students don't have a clear understanding of the different levels of rein contact it takes to achieve softness in the horse. When I'm riding, I use three ways to talk to the horse with my upper body. The first is the most subtle, with just a slight, gentle opening and closing of my fingers on the rein. The second is to use a soft movement of the wrist without changing the position of my arm by my side. This is a difficult movement to teach, as many students break the correct line or rotate their elbows out when they try to move the wrist. Finally, when I want to communicate a stronger message, I take the whole arm back. The elbow moves behind the body, but the position of the body doesn't change so no twisting occurs. In order to do this, my core stays stable and my legs support the position of the horse, so his body can't twist either.

True softness requires a constant dialogue between the horse and rider's leg, seat and hand and this dialogue can only occur when soft rein contact is backed up by a stable core and effective leg control.

stretches in the saddle

As your awareness of your posture and your core stability improves off the horse, you will become better at catching yourself falling into your habitual patterns on the horse. These stretches unlock entrenched patterns and free the body to find a more stable and aligned position. You'll notice that they involve stretching in the opposite direction of your habitual posture. They feel great and you can do them before, during or after a ride.

Slumper reliever

If you have a tendency to slump, simply clasp your hands behind your back, lift your dots and gently lift your arms until you feel a satisfying stretch across the front of your chest. Relax your shoulders and slightly tuck your chin down. Imagine that your arms are lengthening away from your back. Hold for 30 to 60 seconds taking a few deep breaths. Relax and repeat one or two more times.

Swayback reliever

If you're a swayback, cross your hands in front of the body and grab hold of either side of the saddle. Tuck your chin into your chest and round your shoulders and, without moving your hands, pull gently upwards to increase the stretch. You'll feel a lovely pull across your upper back and shoulders. Hold for 30 to 60 seconds, taking a few deep breaths. Relax and repeat one or two more times.

Sideways curve reliever

This stretch has two steps. First, take the arm on the side you curve towards and lift the elbow as high as you can, with your hand pointing down towards the ground. Then, stretch that same arm up and over your head, leaning just slightly over your mid-line. Imagine that your hips are stretching down, away from your long arm, while remaining firmly anchored in the saddle. You'll feel the stretch all down your side. Hold for 30 to 60 seconds taking a few deep breaths while you lengthen the stretch, then relax. You can perform this on both sides to open up the body. Do it first away from your curve, then to the other side and finally do a second stretch away from your curve to fully balance it out.

Stretching tall

This final stretch is for everyone. Start by reaching your arms out in front of you. Place your right hand over your left and close your palms together. Now lift your arms directly over your head, without allowing your back to arch. Keep your spine balanced as you lengthen the arms up and away from the hips. Imagine your hips are sinking down into the saddle, away from your outstretched arms. Relax your shoulders—try not to let them rise up as you stretch. Take a few deep breaths while you hold the stretch. Relax and repeat one or two more times.

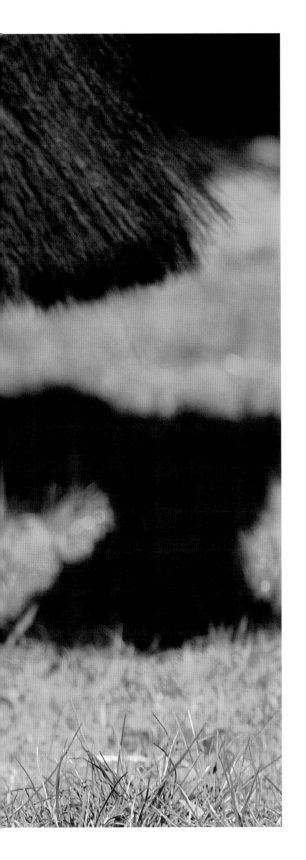

part four
Lifelong
riding

a new way of thinking

A key component of the *Riding from the Inside Out* program is to link the changes that you make in your body to the changes you make in your mind. To begin with you need to develop the physical elements. This is where it is vital to build your understanding of your posture and to work consistently on the appropriate exercises.

But the easiest and yet in some ways perhaps the hardest aspect of the program is changing the way you think about your posture. It's the easiest, because all you have to do catch yourself slipping back to your old habits and use the simple cues we have taught you to correct yourself. It's the hardest because changing a lifetime of poor postural habits takes time, patience and effort. Don't be deterred because it is achievable and the big bonus is you'll begin to see changes in your riding.

Making the commitment to change is an important first step, but following through can be tough. That's because ingrained habits are stubborn and patterns that we've had for a long time feel comfortable. Changing the way your body operates is going to feel strange. At first you'll tire easily as you sit on your newly balanced bottom bones. You'll have to take a break from being aligned, just to let your muscles rest. In fact, sometimes you'll get aches and pains where you've never had them before. This is normal. Think of them as 'good' pains because they mean that you are really working new muscles. It's like starting an exercise program, there are bound to be a few initial complaints! But by sticking at it, the new ways of moving will eventually become automatic. Just how long that will take varies from individual to individual—and depends somewhat on how much you think about it.

Do I have to set aside lots of time to practice?

Absolutely not. The best part of the program is that so much of it involves just going about your normal, everyday activities but in a slightly different way.

An expression I love is, 'You are what you create in your mind.' You can create thought patterns that envisage an aligned, balanced way of standing, sitting and moving and they will become reality not only in the way you sit and stand and move, but in your riding.

What will I feel when I ride?

In the saddle, you'll begin to develop good postural alignment and integrity of movement that never (or rarely) waivers. You won't slump, sway or twist to get a reaction out of your horse. You'll begin to break riding habits that you've had for years and years that may be preventing you from becoming the best rider you can be.

So—not only do you need to get off the horse and do your exercises and stretches to change the way you ride, you need to find a new way of thinking about your body.

What can I do?

There are plenty of opportunities every day to remind yourself of your postural cues. Make sure you are standing firmly on two feet when you are filling the car with petrol or standing in a queue or lift (and throw in a bottom clench for good measure). Don't lean on the sink when you clean your teeth. Keep your spine aligned when you lift your arms in the shower or reach for something on a shelf. Remind yourself to activate your core before you pick up your toddler or a heavy load.

perfect practice off the horse

The key to perfect practice is, not surprisingly, to practise perfectly! It is better for your long-term progress to do small amounts of a given activity perfectly before gradually increasing the challenge. In addition to this important concept, there are three main things to remember when you start to practise your exercises and stretches unmounted. They reinforce each other and provide the consistent feedback required to change your habits.

1 Clever cues
- lift your dots
- balance your bottom bones
- set yourself up on train tracks
- balance your shoulder position
- use your breath
- activate your core

As you **practise** each exercise
ask yourself this:
- Can I be doing this with better alignment?
- Are my dots lifted?
- Are my shoulders in a balanced position?
- Are my feet on train tracks and is my body balanced and aligned?
- Am I using my breath to activate my deep corset?

2 Rest and recover
As soon as you feel your body compensating by losing alignment or balance or wobbling in your centre, or if you feel overly fatigued, stop, rest and either switch to the other side or go to the next movement. You will improve more by doing five or six repetitions perfectly than 20 with poor alignment.

3 Active awareness
This involves developing a sense of how your body feels when you are stretching. While you are stretching first to one side then the other, pay attention to how your body feels. Try to determine which side is tighter. Sometimes you can be given a big hint by noticing how much range of movement you have on one side compared with the other. Remember, doing an extra stretch on the tighter side helps to balance out the body.

Active awareness is a process that you can apply to all your movements both on and off the horse. It's about developing your sense of how you hold your body and building a stronger connection with your physical self that will last for a lifetime of riding.

perfect practice on the horse

Practising perfectly on the horse involves similar elements to practising on terra firma. How-ever, when you ride, it is important not to totally short-circuit your brain with too much infor-mation. Here are some simple steps to help you integrate your off-the-horse training with the real thing.

Choose one element and focus

Don't try to think of everything at once. Pick one cue per ride and make it your focus. During one ride you could think about lifting your dots. On the next one you could think of keeping your shoulders balanced.

Recycle your clever cues

The cues for the exercises and stretches off the horse can be directly applied to your riding sessions. Look through your clever clues before a ride or a lesson and decide which one will be your mantra for that day.

Imprint... then build

Just as new movement patterns are likely to feel strange when you are going about your day, they will do so in the saddle. Try biting off small chunks at a time. Start by maintaining perfect alignment on straighter lines and larger circles. Imprint the feeling of the correct alignment and keep practising it until it begins to become automatic. But don't expect this to happen after one or two rides—we're talking about undoing years of habits. Be prepared for it to take some time before you notice a difference.

Once you have consolidated the feeling of your new balanced alignment, start to challenge it with smaller circles and lateral work. You may find that things start to fall apart pretty quickly with the increased challenges! Apply the concept of perfect practice. Imprint the right pattern even if it is only for a short time.

Don't run before you can crawl

Don't be afraid to take a step back and modify your goals. Remember, when faced with a new challenge the body is likely to revert to old, undesirable habits. It's important to be aware of this if you become despondent when all your hard work seems to disappear whenever you try something new.

In my case, I had been feeling pretty pleased with how my body was responding to the exercises and stretches and Larissa noticed a difference in my riding. I had stopped putting a spur mark on my horse's left side and my improved alignment helped me get him into a better shape, especially in the shoulder-in. So, we started to work on half pass. Going from the centre line to the long side quickly became a battle as I tensed, gripped, tried to force the movement and lost my alignment. I was so worried about getting my horse to move sideways that all my compensation patterns came into play.

So, we changed the goal. I worked on doing half-pass from the long side to the quarter line and I was able to stay better aligned. After imprinting the feeling, I gradually added more challenge. And it's working!

Different challenges, different responses

You'll also find that the different paces of the horse will challenge your new postural stability and alignment. For many riders, it's the sitting trot that presents the most difficult challenge. Attempting to control the movement with your global muscles is one of the greatest obstacles to good sitting trot. If you are gripping and holding on with the big, outer muscles in your body, you will never be able to effectively absorb the movement of the horse. My gripping used to reveal itself as stiffness in my neck and tightness in my jaw—ouch! Not to mention what this said about my ability to move in balance and harmony with my horse…

Each pace offers its own challenges. In rising trot, the body can change its alignment with each up and down rise. This means greater dynamic forces working against stability. In the walk, many riders try to push the horse forward by exaggerating the movement of their seat. This excess movement in the lower body interferes with the soft control that can come from being stable in the centre. And the issues go on…

So, think perfect practice. Do short bursts of work perfectly. As soon as you grip, lose your stirrups, feel tension in your body, pull too hard or notice that your legs are in the wrong spot, go back to the walk. Reestablish your position, think soft, balanced, aligned—and start again.

Sometimes it's better to do this type of practice outside of a formal lesson. Without the pressure of a lesson you can spend time just sitting on your horse, feeling where your body sits in the saddle, noticing the balance and alignment in the walk, then slowly beginning to build the challenges.

damage limitation

Working around horses is hard work. There is always something heavy to lift, carry, pull or move. One of the many benefits of improving your core stability is that it will help you maintain a healthy back, regardless of what you are doing. But a little awareness doesn't go astray and it's important to know that there is a right way and a wrong way to lift and carry. Here's the wrong way to do this.

Lifting a load that is too far away from your body.

Bending over from the waist.

Incorrect

Carrying all the weight on one side of the body.

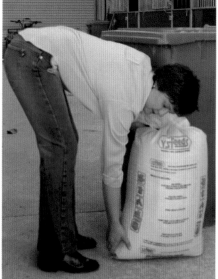

Lifting a heavy object with poor technique.

Make sure you maintain your alignment whenever you're lifting or carrying. Activate your core to minimise the risk of injury to your lower back and think of these key tips.

Bring the object close to the body.

Bend your knees.

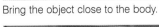

Getting it right

Think of activating your core before you lift heavy objects.

Balance the load on both sides.

putting your program together

Off the horse … for everyone

Alignment

Lift your dots
p 30

Balance your
bottom bones
p 30

Stand evenly
p 21

Stability

Progression

Breathe
p 35

TA awareness
p 37

Standing pelvic
floor
p 41

Leg in/leg out
p 42

Virtual reality
p 44

Strength and control

Bottom clenching
p 70

Deep hip control
p 74

Bent-over row
p 91

Soft arms
p 92

Progression: control with resistance

Standing
p 75

Lying
p 76

Seated
p 77

Horse Simulator
p 94

stretches for your postural type

Stretching off the horse …

Slumper

Table stretch
p 88

Lancelot
p 60

Hamstring stretch
p 64

Lying adductor
p 66

Swayback

Table stretch
p 88

Psoas
p 62

Anti-gravity
hamstring
p 65

On-all-fours
adductor
p 67

Sideways curver

Seated chair twist
p 86

Sitting hip/buttock
p 58

Personalising your program

Regardless of your postural type, everyone should do the alignment, stability, strength and control exercises set out on p 106. Next, add the specific stretches for your postural type. To obtain the full benefit of the program, add the stretches on the horse on p 108.

stretches for your postural type

Stretching on the horse …

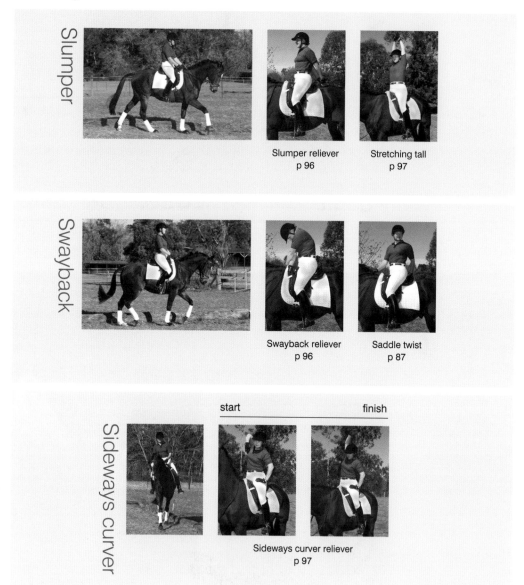

Slumper

Slumper reliever
p 96

Stretching tall
p 97

Swayback

Swayback reliever
p 96

Saddle twist
p 87

Sideways curver

start   finish

Sideways curver reliever
p 97

'A knowledge of the path cannot be substituted
for putting one foot in front of the other.'

MC Richards

acknowledgements

In less than 12 months the concept of Riding from the Inside Out went from being lots of riding lessons, Physiocise sessions, thoughts and ideas to this completed book. Many people have supported the project, but none more than these:

My friend and mentor, Anna-Louise Bouvier, who enlightened me to the workings of my body, who took up virtual riding with such gusto and who shared the innovative work of the Physiocise program.

My amazing coach, Larissa Chadwick, who rides so brilliantly, who put up with all the analysis, who encouraged me in the saddle, and who taught me not to settle for second best in my horse or in myself.

My editor, Jill Brown, who has a gift for fine-tuning and who had sympathy for both the enthusiasm and the worries of a first time author. I could not have found a more encouraging and talented director for the project.

Chris Hector and Roz Neave of the *Horse Magazine* who believed in the concepts and encouraged me to write them down—and to Breanna Chalk who works such magic.

My friend, Maxine Fripp, who encouraged me throughout and allowed us to use her beautiful property, Foxwood, for the photographs.

Designer Ingo Voss who has the patience of a saint and the skill to make it all fit together beautifully.

Julieann Howard who has great photographic talent and patience and who loves the country.

Mary Cerny who is an integral part of my journey.

All my friends in Kangaroo Valley who have been amazing in their support and encouragement, especially to Ruth, our angel.

Nigel who encouraged me to forge ahead, who is an incredible husband and who keeps me grounded and balanced.

And finally our beautiful children, Jessica, Kelsey, Luke and Max, who cooked lots of their own meals, got ready for school without me, made their own fun and waited patiently for Mum to come down from her office. You are our pride and joy.

about the authors

Lisa Champion,
MSc (Exercise Science)

Lisa Champion is an exercise specialist with over 20 years experience in the fitness industry. For the last 15 years she has been one of the directors of the Australian Fitness Network, the professional association for the fitness industry, during which time she has been heavily involved in the training and continuing education of fitness professionals throughout Australia and south-east Asia. In addition, Lisa runs a small personal training business, writes articles for fitness and equestrian publications and is a mother of four. After taking up dressage riding five years ago, she began to link her expertise in the fitness industry with her quest to become a better rider. This link has been the foundation of *Riding from the Inside Out*—the program she has helped to develop with the goal of assisting all riders to improve their postural and movement habits both on and off the horse.

Anna-Louise Bouvier,
MAPA (Physiotherapist)

Anna-Louise Bouvier is a Sydney-based physiotherapist who has developed an innovative and highly effective movement awareness and exercise program called Physiocise to help chronic pain sufferers. The program has been so successful that she has expanded its scope to include the training of elite athletes, fitness professionals, other physios and medical professionals. She has also worked extensively with Qantas, developing an in-flight comfort series for passengers. Her book, *Fix Your Back* (ABC Books 2002), is a national bestseller. Anna-Louise brings careful movement analysis and creative exercise solutions to the *Riding from the Inside Out* program.

Larissa Chadwick,
NCAS Level 1 Coach,
Grand Prix Dressage Rider

Larissa Chadwick won many titles at state and national level in Pony Club before riding her first FEI dressage test at the age of 15. She is now a full-time dressage trainer and coach. Her philosophy of beauty and balance while riding has been a focal point in the development of the principles of the *Riding from the Inside Out* program.

references

Allison G. Joint Position Testing of the Spine: The Role of Feedback in Motor Control Research, 'Proceedings APA WA Biennial State Conference', 2003

Allison G, Kendall et al. 'The Role of the Diaphragm during Abdominal Hollowing Exercises', *Australian Journal of Physiotherapy*, vol 44, no 2, 1998, pp 95–102

Avery, A et al. Utilisation of Transabdominal Ultrasound to Investigate Pelvic Floor Muscles Activity in Males with Lumbo-pelvic Pain, 'Proceedings APA WA Biennial State Conference', 2003

Biering Sorensen F. 'Physical Measurements as Risk Indicators for Low Trouble over a One Year Period', *Spine*, vol 14, 1984, pp 338–344

Deyo RA, Rainville J & Kent DL. What Can the History and Physical Examination Tell Us about Low Back Pain?' *JAMA* 1992, vol 286, pp 760–765

Butler DS & Moseley GL. *Explain Pain*, Noigroup Publications, Adelaide, 2003

Faas A. 'Exercises: Which Ones are Worth Trying, for Which Patients and When?' *Spine*, vol 21, 1996, pp 2874-2879

Frost H et al. 'A Fitness Program for Patients with Chronic Low Back Pain: A 2-Year Follow-up of a Randomised Controlled Trial', *Pain*, vol 75, 1998, pp 273–279

Hides JA, Richardson CA & Jull GA. 'Multifidus Muscle Recovery is not Automatic after Resolution of Acute First Episode Low Back Pain', *Spine*, vol 21, no 23, 1996, pp 2763–2769

Hides JA et al. Multifidus Muscle Rehabilitation Decreases Recurrence of Symptoms following First Episode Low Back Pain. 'Proceeding of the National Physiotherapy Congress', 1996, pp 43–45

Hides JA et al. 'Evidence of Lumbar Multifidus Muscle Wasting Ipsilateral to Symptoms in Patients with Acute/Sub-acute Low Back Pain', *Spine*, vol 19, no 2, 1994, pp 165–172, JB Lippencott Company

Hodges P. Dealing with the changes to spinal stability: the mechanisms of motor control of the trunk. 'Proceedings of the Seventh Scientific Conference of the IFOMT (2000) in conjunction with the MPAA', pp 206–215

Hodges PW. Top to Bottom: Integrating Science and Practice for Cardiothoracics, Womens Health, Neurology and Musculoskeletal Physiotherapy, 'Proceedings APA WA Biennial State Conference', 2003

Hodges PW. The Brain, Pain, Muscles and Joint Stability: Fitting the Puzzle Together. 'Proceedings of the Fifth Annual International APA Congress', 1998, pp 108–111

Hodges PW & Richardson CA. 'Inefficient Muscular Stabilisation of the Lumbar Spine Associated with Low Back Pain: A Motor Control Evaluation of Transversus Abdominis', *Spine*, vol 21, 1996, pp 2640-2650

Hodges PW. Current Opinion of the Function of Transversus Abdominis. An Annotated Bibliography of Papers Investigating Transversus Abdominis, Manual Therapy Special Group Newsletter 3, November 1998, pp 8–11

Hodges PW & Richardson CA. 'Contraction of the Abdominal Muscles Associated with Movement of the Lower Limb', *Physical Therapy*, vol 77, 1997, pp 132–144

Indahl A, Velund L & Reikeraas O. 'Good Prognosis for Low Back Pain when Left Untampered', *Spine*, vol 20, 1995, pp 473–477

Jemmet R. *Spinal Stabilisation: The New Science of Back Pain*, 2E, Novont Health Publishing, Halifax, Canada, 2003

Keer, R & Grahame, R. *The Hypermobility Syndrome*, Butterworths Heinemann, Edinburgh, 2003

Lord S & Castell S. 'Effect of Exercise on Balance, Strength and Reaction Time in Older People', *Australian Journal of Physiotherapy*, vol 40, no 2, 1994, pp 83–88

McGill, S. *Low Back Disorders: Evidence-Based Prevention and Rehabilitation*, Human Kinetics Publishers, Champaign, Ill, USA, 2003

Mulder T. Current Motor Control Theories: Implications for Rehabilitation, 'Proceedings of the Fifth Annual International APA Congress', 1998, pp 92-94

Noe DA, Mostardi RA, Jackson ME, Portersfield JA & Askew MJ. 'Myoelectric Activity and Sequencing of Selected Trunk Muscles during

Isokinetic Lifting', *Spine*, vol 17, no 2, 1992, p 225

O'Sullivan P et al. 'Altered Motor Control Strategies in Subjects with Sacroiliac Joint Pain during Active Straight Leg Raise Test, *Spine*, vol 27, no 1, 2002, E1–E8

O'Sullivan PB, Twomey L & Allison G. 'Dysfunction of the Neuro-Muscular System in the Presence of Back Pain: Implications for Physical Therapy Management', *Journal of Manual and Manipulative Therapy*, vol 5, no 1, 1997, pp 20–26

O'Sullivan PB, Twomey L et al. 'Altered Patterns of Abdominal Muscle Activation in Patients with Chronic Low back Pain', *Australian Journal of Physiotherapy*, vol 43, no 2, 1997

Panjabi M, Abumi K, Duranceau J & Oxland T. 'Spinal Stability and Intersegmental Muscle Forces: A Biomechanical Model', *Spine*, vol 4, no 2, 1989, pp 194–200

Panjabi M. 'The Stabilising System of the Spine: Part 1, Function, Dysfunction, Adaptation and Enhancement', *Journal of Spinal Disorders*, vol 5, no 4, 1992, pp 383–389

Panjabi M. 'The Stabilising System of the Spine: Part 11, Neutral Zone and Instability Hypothesis', *Journal of Spinal Disorders*, vol 5, 1992, pp 390-397

Quint U & Wilkie HJ. 'Importance of the Intersegmental Trunk Muscles for the Stability of the Lumbar Spine: A Biomechanical Study, *Spine*, vol 23, no 18, 1998, pp 1937–1945

Sahrmann SA. Diagnosis and Treatment of Movement-related Pain Syndromes Associated with Muscle and Movement Imbalances, Course Manual, 1997

Shacklock MO. 'Central Pain Mechanisms. A New Horizon in Manual Therapy', *Australian Journal of Physiotherapy*, vol 45, 1999, pp 83–92

Vleeming A et al. A New Light on Low Back Pain: The Self-locking Mechanism of the Sacroiliac Joints and its Implications for Sitting, Standing and Walking, 'Proceedings of the Fifth Annual International APA Congress', 1998, pp 57–76

audio CD overview

Join Anna-Louise Bouvier as she talks you through key exercises in *Riding from the Inside Out*, giving you directions for the correct set-up, timing and execution of each one. We recommend that you have your book handy and refer to the photographs to make sure you are doing them correctly.

resources

Exercise bands and fitballs can be sourced from sports and fitness shops and websites

Visit **www.ridingfromtheinsideout.com**
- for information on workshops
- and for links to related sites